CULTURAL SEXISM

The Politics of Feminist Rage in the
#MeToo Era

Heather Savigny

BRISTOL
UNIVERSITY
PRESS

First published in Great Britain in 2020 by

Bristol University Press
University of Bristol
1-9 Old Park Hill
Bristol
BS2 8BB
UK
t: +44 (0)117 954 5940
pp-info@bristol.ac.uk
www.bristoluniversitypress.co.uk

© Bristol University Press 2020

British Library Cataloguing in Publication Data
A catalogue record for this book is available from the British Library.

ISBN 978-1-5292-0644-9 hardcover
ISBN 978-1-5292-0647-0 ePub
ISBN 978-1-5292-0646-3 ePdf

Cover design: blu inc, Bristol
Cover image credit: Christopher Campbell/unsplash
Printed and bound in Great Britain by CPI Group (UK)
Ltd, Croydon, CR0 4YY
Policy Press uses environmentally responsible print
partners.

To Simon, Sam and Krissy. Thank you.

Contents

Introduction:
From Waves to Tsunamis

On 5 October 2017, the *New York Times* ran with the headline 'Harvey Weinstein paid off sexual harassment accusers for decades'.[1] On 15 October 2017, actress Alyssa Milano tweeted, 'If you've been sexually harassed or assaulted write "me too" as a reply to this tweet'. By the following day, #MeToo had been tweeted more than 500,000 times.[2] Women were speaking out publicly about the abuse and harassment that they had been subjected to – and they were being believed. When #MeToo first began to appear in media conversations and news headlines it was harrowing to hear those stories. But there was also a sense of optimism. Could we be seeing the end of this kind of behaviour towards women? We were reminded how brave those women were for speaking out. Perpetrators were being fired, Harvey Weinstein was being accused of sexual misconduct, and it seemed that we may have been on the cusp of a fundamental cultural shift, where to harass, assault and abuse women was no longer part of what was considered, by some, to be acceptable.

However, two years after this, there are questions as to what #MeToo has achieved. An article published in *The Guardian* in 2019 quoted Zelda Perkins, a former assistant of Harvey Weinstein, as saying: 'People are beginning to speak and the water is stirring, but I don't think that the changes are as big as people would have hoped in the two-year period. When you think about how shocking all the information that we have received – and are still receiving – is, unfortunately people have already been slightly inured to it'.[3]

This book explores the points raised in this quotation. #MeToo caught the public imagination and garnered much media attention about the abuse, assault and harassment of women, in a way that had previously been relatively marginal. But what we also know is that what these women were speaking about was nothing new. Literature in general and feminist writing in particular is full of examples of women speaking about a range of abuses that they have been subjected to. So my starting point involves perhaps more fundamental questions: will anything really change as a result of #MeToo? What is it that is stopping the sort of change people had initially hoped for?

This book is an academic exploration of these issues, but it is also a personal book. I wish I could say I knew women, or indeed, even a woman, who has not had her own #MeToo moment. The ubiquity of sexual assault and harassment in the workplace reaches way beyond Hollywood superstars. Talk to any woman and sooner or later you will hear her experience: an experience, or cumulative experiences, that have defined her place in the world. During my career, and in my personal life, I have witnessed the aftermath and seen the damage done to women not only by men's abuse, but also by the consequences of speaking out about that abuse. These consequences range from self-blame, to impacts on relationships, health and professional prospects. Women's bravery in speaking out is in tension with the *impact* not only of assault, but of the attempts to silence, disbelieve or minimize her speech about that assault which follow.

We now have a generation of women who better understand their rights and the boundaries that they are entitled to protect. Nonetheless, stories like this make us angry and the system that perpetuates such abuse makes us angry. So how do we turn this rage into something that is creative, constructive and political? This question underpins not only the discussion and examples within the book but my own act of writing, theorizing and reflecting on this moment in time as political. It is also an act of creative feminist rage.

It has taken me a while to get to this point of being able to channel that rage creatively and this has not been an overnight story. My background in political science was in an academic discipline very much concerned with 'objectivity': being angry was something that was not a feature of our analytical toolkit. Politics as a subject matter was often defined very narrowly in terms of state actors and institutions (such as legislatures and assemblies). But to make sense of the ways in which we as citizens have our perceptions of what takes place in these institutions shaped, I turned to media and cultural studies. From feminist theorizing what I also learned was almost intuitive: politics takes place every time there is a power relationship, be that in the family home, or the interactive relationship between media and political elites. This book is concerned with capturing and illustrating these power structures and the political ways in which they are made manifest through reference to Westernized mediated cultural sources, rather than seeking to quantify the unquantifiable nature of patriarchy.[4] Because it is only once we are able to grasp the physically ungraspable nature of our cultural context that we can really understand what politics is. Once we do that we can repoliticize these debates around sexism, highlighting the underlying power structures that inform what we do see. In so doing we can also creatively use our rage and anger to effect change.

Women who have made complaints are often subjected to further violence, when they are not believed, when sexual predators remain in the workplace, or convictions are not secured. And this is something that we see repeated time and again. Patriarchal power structures are reinforced through the message that is being sent by organizations and legal structures that you can be a sexual predator and get away with it. But these messages serve to further traumatize a woman who has survived an assault, and those around her who wish to support her in the aftermath. That women are still having these experiences, not only in workplaces but in social spaces and in the street, requires an understanding of how this type of behaviour is culturally legitimated in the first place. How is it that sexism is so ingrained in our cultural psyche and our social structures that these types of behaviour, and those exposed through #MeToo, have been hidden (in plain sight) for so long? We have a history of feminist activism, writing, thinking and ways of being and so it is disingenuous and simplistic to suggest that #MeToo provides something completely different. But what it does do is shine a spotlight on issues that women have talked about historically and helps us realize that this is something that we still have to tackle. It also helps us realize that it is okay to be angry and to reflect on how we can use this constructively and in a way that does not cause us further harm.

This book is about working out, how and why, in an era that we might even call post-#MeToo, very little seems to have changed structurally. Sexism is still embedded in our cultural structures, industries, and the values that shape our Western societies. Some of this lies in the role that media play in our lives, shaping and framing how we view and make sense of the world. It is also about the role of politics in our daily lives and about the history that has come to shape and define who we are, and who we see ourselves as. For many in the UK, these structures and ideas that shape our lives are predominantly masculinized and predominantly white. And there have been some excellent books that explore British history and include people of colour and their contributions (see for example Afua Hirsch; Akala; Benjamin Zephaniah; and Reni Eddo-Lodge to name but a few).[5] However, we are living in an era where not only has race been at times written out of the #MeToo discussion, but so has the history of feminist theorizing. Feminists have been to prison and risked their lives to fight for the rights that women have today. The freedoms that we have are a consequence of women standing up, speaking collectively, and getting angry.

#MeToo, and the wider phenomena it speaks to, reminds us that from the micro aggressions to the harassment and assault, women are being harmed both physically and in their silencing, isolation and loss of self-belief. As Dale Spender argues, we really do need to think about what men have done to women and the ideas that they have had.[6] #MeToo is by no means the first time women's interests and rights have been at stake. And the history of feminism reminds us that women have battled, successfully, to change things. (For a wonderful development of this see Karen Boyle's *#MeToo, Weinstein & Feminism*.[7]) What we need to do is to understand how patriarchy has reinvented itself, and so successfully. Undoing the sexism which underpins our cultures requires an understanding of just how it has become so embedded within our culture, and an understanding of how sexism is manifested despite the successful battles that women have fought. What follows in this introduction is intended to set the scene for some of the issues and debates from within feminist thought that underpin the discussion that takes place throughout this book.

Feminism

The term feminism first appeared in the late 1880s. This was the term for that which had previously been referred to as women's rights. The fight for women to be treated equally and as independent beings in their own rights has a long history. Aphra Behn was one of the earliest English women to have made a living from writing and to speak out about conditions for women. Her play, written in 1670, *The Forc'd Marriage*, is often seen as one of the first public explorations of the dominance of men. Moreover, seen as radical at the time, she also advocated equality of women. Her work set the scene for centuries of responses to women speaking up and speaking out; the play was met with dismissal and anger by the male-dominated literary establishment.[8] If we fast forward just over 100 years, in 1792 Mary Wollstonecraft also put forward a critique of the male established order, a direct critique inspired by Thomas Paine's *Vindication of the Rights of Man*. In *A Vindication of the Rights of Woman* she argued that women needed to be educated equally, in order that they would be able to gain, and be eligible for, equal rights. She offered a critique of the prevailing conventional wisdom: '"Educate women like men," says Rousseau, "and the more they resemble our sex the less power will they have over us." This is the very point I aim at. I do not wish them to have power over men; but over themselves'.[9] In so doing, her argument neatly challenged both the irrational male fears that underpinned the then systems of education from which women were excluded, and made a powerful case for women's equality.

But it took over 70 years from the time of Wollstonecraft's writing for women to gain access to higher education. A campaign begun by Sophia Jex-Blake in 1869 resulted in her and six other women being able to sit the matriculation exams in order to enter the University of Edinburgh to study medicine. Her protest was initiated by a newspaper advert asking for other women to come and sit the exam, after the University had rejected her original solo application on the grounds that it could not make arrangements 'in the interest of one lady'.[10] Sophia Jex-Blake and the Edinburgh Seven thus started a campaign which resulted in the successful change to legislation and allowed for women to apply for admission to study in universities. This had previously been denied on grounds such as that women's brains were smaller than men's; that a woman's education would do damage to her femininity; and of course, the strain that this might put on men in having to teach women.[11]

The story of women's feminism is often presented in 'waves'. Not only were women fighting to be educated, but Wollstonecraft's work and the movements of the middle classes (mainly women) in the 18th and 19th centuries formed the foundations of what has been termed the 'first wave' of feminism. This culminated in Britain in the form of the Suffragettes movement in the early 20th century. Subjected to state violence (such as being imprisoned and force-fed by authorities) the Suffragette movement fought for the enfranchisement of women. The battles of the first wave feminists are often presented as revolving around one issue: the vote. The furore and reaction in public discourse to this demand for political equality is discussed in more detail in Chapter 3. But suffice to say it was a period of brutality against women and 126 years went by after the publication of *A Vindication of the Rights of Woman* before some women in Britain got the right to vote in 1918. In this reading, first wave feminism was primarily concerned with political equality through legislation. However, as philosopher and activist Emma Goldman observed at the time, despite enfranchisement political equality was not a given for women.[12] As will be discussed in more detail in Chapter 2, the origins of inequality and sexism had far deeper roots, and a much wider reach.

Becoming enfranchised however, had not meant an end to all other forms of political, economic and social inequality that women were subject to. The beginnings of the 'second wave' are often thought to be grounded in Betty Friedan's *The Feminine Mystique* published in 1963. The term 'second wave' was first used in a *New York Times* article in 1968, to describe American women who wished to disassociate themselves from the (male-dominated) new left movement in the US which had become prominent in the 1960s.[13] Friedan's work was concerned with the ways in which middle-class women were subject to 'the problem with no name'; the public private split and the expectations that they marry, become mothers, housewives and adjuncts of men, with little or no autonomy of their own. Her work was subjected to extensive critique for being focused only on the interests of white middle-class women (for who would be doing the childcare and housework if these women were at work?). This was the critique of an economic system which relied on women's reproductive capacities as a mechanism to exploit them, as Shulamith Firestone argued in *The Dialectic of Sex*.[14] And if one woman's emancipation relied on another woman's exploitation then clearly there was something wrong with the system. Moreover, not only were there structural issues at stake in the fight for both liberty and equality, but cultural ones too. Simone de Beauvoir's claim that 'one is not born, but rather becomes, a woman' is perhaps the most oft cited and most illustrative example of the challenges to the cultural norms of a society structured around biological difference as a justification for masculine dominance.[15] (This issue is also discussed in more detail in Chapter 2.)

Second wave feminists, such as radical feminists Catharine MacKinnon and Andrea Dworkin, also battled for women's rights over their bodies.[16] Catharine MacKinnon's work was influential in getting the term, and the act of, sexual harassment recognized in legislation. Crucially, she provided a language – a vocabulary to talk about the very real abuse that women were suffering in the workplace – and challenged the structures that had enabled this. Dworkin expanded these parameters to explore the ways in which sexual violence was normalized within the pornography industry and the domination and humiliation of women was eroticized for the pleasure of men. In essence they pointed to the ways in which media, cultural industries and legal structures normalized and perpetuated an assumption of control over women's bodies. For example, Leslie Reagan shows us how the *Roe v. Wade* ruling, which decriminalized abortion, was a logical response to decades of pressure from pioneering women such as MacKinnon and Dworkin fighting for birth control, contraception, and ownership and control over their own bodies.[17] This is something which, as we see at the time of writing, is an issue that needs to be revived given the 2019 signing of legislation that made abortion illegal in Alabama. It is concerning that this also suggests an undoing of the gains and advancements of feminism per se. It seems that men still think in myriad ways (because this is an issue right at the heart of #MeToo) that they have the right to control, and to determine what happens to, women's bodies. Our bodies. However, while second wave feminism gave women a voice, critiques developed which highlighted how this version of feminism spoke only to, and for, some.

In 1851 Sojourner Truth attended a Woman's Rights Convention in Ohio. On 23 April 1863 the story of her speaking up was reported by Frances Dana Gage in an article in *The Independent* (New York). Gage had chaired the event where she had ignored demands that Sojourner Truth not be allowed to speak. Gage invited her up on stage and Sojourner Truth gave a speech that has become legendary within feminism since the 19th century:

> Dat man over dar say dat woman needs to be helped in to carriages, and lifted over ditches, and to have de best place eberywhar. Nobody eber helps me into carriages, or ober mud puddles, or gives me any best place. And ar'n't I a woman. Look at me. Look at my arm [baring her arm to show her muscular power] I have plowed and planted and gathered into barns, and no man could head me – and ar'n't I a woman?[18]

As Nell Irvin Painter goes on to argue, in the exhibiting of her right arm, not only does she demonstrate her equality with men, but she figuratively also rescues white women and carries them to safety. The symbolism of a woman bearing her arm has long since been used within feminist imagery, although the raced dimension of this feminist act has often been erased. These days we are much more likely to see the image of white women baring their arms used in campaign messages and images around feminism, rather than the originator of this symbolism, who was Black. And it is this erasure of race within feminism that was at the heart of one of the most significant divisions within second wave feminism. While authors such as Betty Friedan and Germaine Greer were writing about predominantly white middle-class women, bell hooks and Audre Lorde wrote powerfully about the interests of Black women. They drew on Truth's incredible testimony and argued that their histories and interests also needed to be taken seriously and recognized. In her essay *The Master's Tools Will Never Dismantle the Master's House,* Audre Lorde wrote that by denying the differences between women, white feminism simply perpetuated the raced sexism that patriarchy required to maintain its own existence. In this sense, white women became complicit in the continuation of sexism in failing to recognize this difference. This important observation was perhaps most clearly articulated by Kimberlé Crenshaw in her analysis of the legal treatment of a number of Black, working-class women in a US factory and the refusal – on the grounds of race or gender – of their claim for equal treatment. What Crenshaw argued was that these women were discriminated against twice: on the grounds of race *and* gender. It was at this 'intersection' where the injustice was done (again, this is explored in more detail in Chapter 2).

The 'third wave' of feminism can be seen as defining and describing two almost diametrically opposed positions. In the 1980s and 1990s, on the one hand there was the encouragement to adopt the view that there was no longer a need for feminism; on the other hand, scholars such as Susan Faludi, Angela McRobbie and Ros Gill pointed us towards the 'backlash' and re-emergence of ironic sexism. And so it is the case that often the history of feminism is presented as having taken place in 'waves': the first wave associated with voting rights; the 'second wave' wave with equality in legislation; the third wave with sex positivity and a younger generation of women (some argued that we were in a post-feminist era). Most recently, #MeToo has been associated with a 'fourth wave' feminism mainly revolving around technology (blogs and social media platforms such as Twitter and Instagram) as a mechanism where young women can have a voice and engage in activism. Celebrities such as Beyoncé and Emma Watson are proudly displaying their feminist credentials and engaging younger generations in the normalizing of the need for women to have their rights and interests taken seriously. On the one hand the notion of waves enables a clear and quick snapshot of progression and suggests that things are moving forward and getting better. However, on the other hand, this presentation also suggests that some of these battles are no longer necessary. Yet, #MeToo (and wider associated campaigns such as Time's Up) has shown us that Catharine MacKinnon's writings around sexual harassment are still relevant today, albeit well beyond the workplace.

The history of feminism has also often been written in our media narratives as women being antagonistic towards each other. But this is a woeful and convenient patriarchal inaccuracy. It is possible for women to have a range of views that reflect their own interests, and still collectively unite to fight the variety of ways in which the patriarchy reinvents itself as patriarchies. The use of waves to describe feminist history suggests to us notions of peak points and then progress. The use of waves as a metaphor has served to suggest a discrete period of change. However, waves are actually, literally, peak points of water just going round and round. They are little shifts in the sand, and these waves ebb away too. In this sense, the characterizing of the history of feminism in waves becomes simply another mechanism to prevent women's progress being fully realized. The making explicit of women's activism and gains in the telling of the #MeToo campaign has the potential to situate this moment within another wave of feminist history. If we want to see this achieve more than be part of a wave that ebbs and flows, then, as I argue in the conclusion, what we need is a tsunami.

These men and masculinity

The way that we tell stories about women's achievements matters. Not only because it reminds us of the significance of women's ideas and interests, but also because it encourages us to think about how those stories get told. Virginia Woolf highlights the difference between the widely celebrated Shakespeare, who was encouraged to travel and write, and Jane Austen, unable to travel and who had to hide her work from her visitors. Writing nearly 100 years ago, she observed that:

The most transient visitor to this planet, I thought, who picked up this [news]paper could not fail to be aware, even from this scattered testimony, that England is under the rule of a patriarchy. Nobody in their senses could fail to detect the dominance of the professor. His was the power the money and the influence. He was the proprietor of the paper and its editor and sub-editor. He was the Foreign Secretary and the Judge. He was the cricketer; he owned the racehorses and the yachts. He was the director of the company that pays two hundred per cent to its shareholders. He left millions to charities and colleges that were ruled by himself. He suspended the film actress in mid-air ... with the exception of the fog he seemed to control everything.[19]

She highlighted the prominence and dominance of men and men's interests across society. We might ask how much and how little has changed since this observation. To repoliticize sexism is about listening to that range of experiences and exploring how it is that we come to hold the views about women that we do today. In understanding how we talk about women, it is perhaps useful to briefly reflect on how we talk and think about men.

As I suggest throughout this book, our media narratives oftentimes encourage us to ignore the achievements of women beyond a narrow idealized assumption of womanhood, and they also invite us to celebrate a particular kind of man. So when we talk about men, much as when we talk about women, there are clearly a diversity of men and male behaviour and responses. Just as there is not a one-size-fits-all definition of 'woman' nor does the same hold for 'man'. But if we collapse these distinctions what are we left with? Is it possible to consider exploitation and subordination of women, without an understanding of 'man'? The literature around gender is particularly useful in making sense of this. R.W. Connell developed the term 'hegemonic masculinity'.[20] What this concept did was acknowledge differences between men (for example, in terms of race and sexuality) and highlight the ways in which it is a particular type of masculinity that has come to be defined as the norm. This type of masculinity is linked to wealth and social status and translates broadly into the characteristics of the white, wealthy, heterosexual, upper/middle-class male. Crucially, this version of masculinity relies on a confidence and a sense of entitlement; an entitlement to wealth, money and power. In the UK, we might observe this type of expression of masculinity in many of our white male Eton/public school-educated MPs. This 'alpha male' type of masculinity is also connected with an assumption of entitlement to women's bodies as will be discussed throughout the book. Although Connell did not directly draw this out, it is argued here that it is that real sense of entitlement which underpins this particular kind of masculinity; the assumption that the world works in the interests of this particular type of man, to the point where deviations from this kind of world view become positioned as 'identity politics' and trivialized (as I discuss in the following chapter). White, heterosexual, upper/middle-class men also have an identity. It is just that theirs is the one that has shaped our politics to such an extent that this identity is so ingrained as to be assumed to be the 'natural order of things' rather than an expression of identity in its own right.

I also want to suggest in this book that this entitlement identity is encapsulated in the language of merit and in contemporary neoliberalism (as discussed in Chapter 4). For Connell, the way in which this understanding of masculinity became normalized, hegemonic, so taken for granted and ultimately 'common sense', was through its relational positioning with what it meant to be a woman. The construction of this type of masculinity was dependent upon a system of oppression and domination of woman. For masculinity to be realized, and superior, the oppositional position of woman was that of inferiority. As with other feminist and cultural theorizing, masculinity was reliant on the inferiority of the feminine 'other'.[21]

Connell is keen to point out that this version of masculinity is about a system of privilege rather than individual men (many of whom are also uncomfortable with this positioning, which we might see illustrated by #NotAllMen). Indeed, it may well be only a minority of men who enact this type of masculinity.[22] At the same time, we also see some women enact the features of this type of hegemonic masculinity; an identity underpinned by an assumption of entitlement. However, what the term 'hegemonic masculinity' also does is enable us to unpack how 'particular groups of men inhabit positions of power and wealth, and how they legitimate and reproduce the social relationships that generate their dominance'.[23] That is, once we see that there is an identity politics of white, upper/middle-class, heterosexual men, we can see how the world around them is structured to work in their interests. Their identity politics relies on this sense of entitlement to this positioning in the world. So when I talk about men in this book, I am talking about this type of masculinity, embodied in *these* men. These are the men who express the 'right kind' of masculinity, the identity politics of entitlement, and who uphold and benefit from a system designed around their interests (and the women who enable them). I am not talking about the men who 'get it' and work to advance women's interests, and speak up and out for a diversity of women. I do not want to essentialize men and women, and so find this formulation helpful in making sense of these categories of gender. Because if we remove the vocabulary of men and women, we make the outcome of this relationship, patriarchy, invisible. So, when I use the term 'men' I am using it to reflect those with privilege and a sense of entitlement who play a key role in sustaining the entitled, masculinized, patriarchal version of the world that we live in today.

Key arguments of this book

Ultimately, this is about exposing the sexism embedded in our Western cultures, identifying and defining it for what it is: cultural sexism. This book is also concerned with harnessing feminist rage as a mechanism to explore and consider, why, despite the history of feminism, we are still in a position where something like #MeToo was necessary.

The book will show, first, why structures fail women and how sexism and misogyny are embedded within our Western cultural systems. That is to say, the way that we are given to understand the world around us and the society we live in is shaped not only by legislation but in and through our mediated culture. Media have the capacity to shape our norms and values. And it is that norm and value shaping that will be unpacked and exposed within this book; structures fail, it will be argued, because of the cultural legitimation of sexism.

Second, I will argue that the identification of this cultural sexism needs to be harnessed creatively as a mechanism for social and political change. This is a book about repoliticizing sexism, and recognizing the role of media in this process of cultural embedding, so that we can use feminist rage creatively to undo these structures and cultures that serve to legitimate the violation and subordination of women.

In focusing our attention only on #MeToo itself as a 'media event' sexism and misogyny are depoliticized. This is publicity not politics; media narratives which take the politics out of #MeToo obscure power structures and mean that we miss the opportunity for change. #MeToo can function as a catalyst to repoliticize issues of sexism. #MeToo has given voice to the experiences of huge numbers of women and these voices reveal patterns and trends. Media narratives that have focused on individual stories have served simply to depoliticize the underlying sexism that gave rise to the need to speak out about these experiences. They hide the structures of power and patriarchy/ies in which sexism is embedded. Changing our mediated power structures requires cultural change. Media coverage of #MeToo has been less focused on those women who are not celebrities; what about the cleaners, the school kids, the coffee shop workers? Will their experiences really change due to this media exposure? It seems unlikely while we live in a densely sexualized cultural context and our cultural output remains derived from the male gaze.[24] Plot lines in films and TV shows show rape as a normal part of our daily cultural lives.[25] Calls for the advertising industry to reflect on the harms caused by underlying sexism have been met with belittling responses which demean and undermine the very micro-level experiences of 'Everyday Sexism'.[26] As Laura Bates' extremely powerful work on the Everyday Sexism Project has demonstrated, these harms which in isolation may be very small (or not) cumulatively form a cultural backdrop, which legitimizes and normalizes sexism and its manifestation in sexual assault, harassment, violence and abuse.[27] We need to ask some urgent questions about the cultural climate that we live in which sees one in three women worldwide subjected to sexual violence[28], and where women continue to be murdered by their male partners[29].

What #MeToo and the history of feminism have shown is that speaking out can effect change. The agency that I see in women around me is incredibly powerful; young women especially have a strength and a voice that I did not have all those years ago. As they navigate a social media environment filled with images and ideals of perfection, and a sexist world around them, it is them, for me, who are the real agents of change; the young women across the world who aren't going to put up with this, and believe that the world really can and should be a better place for them. The book ends with a reflection on how this agency can be extended constructively through repoliticization and the harnessing of rage.

Conclusion

It is fundamentally depressing to think that people have become inured, and are no longer shocked by, appalling levels of abuse, harassment and assault against women, as Zelda Perkins (in the quote at the start of this chapter) suggests has happened. This book is an attempt to explore *why* this inuring of shock at abuse has happened. To do that we need to look beyond the events of #MeToo itself, and explore how the political and social structures around us in the West have played a key role in creating a culture which legitimizes, normalizes and trivializes abuse of women. How then do we change this, and politicize the cultural structures that normalize these experiences? I am arguing here that repoliticizing sexism means refusing to be defined by existing narratives of white male entitlement and superiority. This is a political act. To repoliticize sexism, we need to expose it and use our understanding of how it works to undo and change our cultural structures. The media play a fundamental role in shaping the environment that we are in, shaping our norms and values of what is and is not legitimate. There is nuance, and it is not just the goalposts that have moved for women, but the whole football pitch has shifted to accommodate the changing, evolving nature of sexism and patriarchy. To undo this, we need to expose how sexism has become embedded, and think about how we can act collectively to make a difference.

Sexism is systemic and systematic. It is so ingrained in our society that it will take more than the euphoric period of optimism that flowed from #MeToo bringing conversations about sexual abuse and harassment into the public eye. #MeToo is not enough if it is simply part of another 'wave'; a wave that reaches peak moment, and then results in us being marginally further forward than we were before. Waves do not shift the whole beach or change the landscape; we need a tsunami. If we want to change the landscape we need a more comprehensive conversation about how and why this sexism has become so ingrained that some men (and women) cannot even see it. They cannot see the problem with their behaviour (as evidenced perhaps by those men who are seeking to return to their high-profile or even just normal careers after their period of exclusion from the public realm). In essence, I argue that we need to expose the political nature of the power dynamics that sustain and enable the reinvention of patriarchal structures.

This book is also itself a moment of political action, exploring those underlying cultural mechanisms which contextualize the sexism that has been exposed by #MeToo, and considering how and why these experiences and moments have become so unremarkable; they have become depoliticized. Repoliticizing this sexism, by exposing the politics and power relations that sustain patriarchal structures, means that these individual moments of women speaking up contain the possibility of a fundamental landscape shift.

1

Repoliticizing

The #MeToo campaign has been powerful, long overdue and immensely important. It has heightened awareness of the ways in which women are subjected to sexual assault, harassment and abuse; and, as also evidenced by Laura Bates's Everyday Sexism Project, for a lot of women this takes place on a daily basis. So what do we do with this cumulative knowledge? And what have we learned? It would seem that we have been reminded of the sheer power of women speaking up collectively. This collective voice, in all of its diverse forms, does have the capacity to reshape the landscape. We have also seen that some women are being believed. But how do we ensure that all women have the opportunity to give voice to their experiences, and moreover, not be subjected to them in the first place? To ask these questions is to ask about the nature of power and the way in which it is structured, maintained and evolves within our society. To ask questions about the way in which power works is to ask political questions.[1] To ask political questions is to ask who benefits from the power relationship? Who wins and loses?

What the #MeToo movement, and its forerunner MeToo exposes are the ways in which women lose out in a system which is structured around particular kind of masculine interests (those of white, heterosexual, middle/upper-class men with a sense of entitlement) and their preservation. These men (as discussed in the introduction) stand to benefit in our current Western and capitalist structures. As will be noted in the following chapter this is nothing new. And if these structures of power are nothing new, then what #MeToo and the issues it brings to the table will highlight are the ways in which these masculinized power structures have evolved to maintain this type of domination (which also disadvantages men who do not fit the 'mould').

To inform this discussion, this chapter reflects on the emergence of the MeToo movement and the #MeToo campaign as bringing to light the wider phenomenon of sexism that is part of the society that we live in, and which manifests itself in a range of differing ways. Underlying this chapter, and indeed the whole book, is a political questioning of the expression and nature of this masculinized power: how and why has this sexist behaviour with implied assumptions about what women are *for* become so taken for granted, so normal? How is it that the abuse and harassment of women is something which has been (and is seen as) acceptable? Many individuals have been named as perpetrators as survivors have come forward to describe their experiences. Some individuals have been removed from their positions of power and public influence (while some have not). However, I would suggest that when media narratives focus only on individuals as perpetrators, we witness the depoliticization of the issues that MeToo/#MeToo raise more widely. In essence, my intention is to suggest that in order to challenge the cultural sexism that has become embedded and normalized we need to repoliticize sexism. To repoliticize sexism means that we need to ask questions about how and why MeToo/#MeToo was necessary in the first place.

MeToo

Tarana Burke had run a summer camp. At this camp she and the young girls attending told their stories of abuse and assault. These stories were horrifying and distressing, and they mobilized her to create the MeToo campaign. Launching in 2007, her aim was to raise awareness and consciousness of the pain that women are subjected to, and the strength that they display in the face of this. It was a campaign of support and solidarity. Her campaign led with her reflection on a story shared with her by a young girl on that camp, a survivor of sexual assault. Burke wrote:

> I could not find the courage that she had found.
> I could not muster the energy to tell her that I

understood, that I connected, that I could feel her pain. I couldn't help her release her shame, or impress upon her that nothing that happened to her was her fault. I could not find the strength to say out loud the words that were ringing in my head over and over again as she tried to tell me what she had endured … I watched her walk away from me as she tried to recapture her secrets and tuck them back into their hiding place. I watched her put her mask back on and go back into the world like she was all alone and I couldn't even bring myself to whisper … **me too**.[2]

Her words articulate the helplessness and feeling of fellowship that so many experience in hearing of women's suffering and pain at the hands of men in a system that goes on allowing this to happen. Her words are profound in terms of the depths of despair that they articulate. They also encourage us to be empathetic readers, and acknowledge and recognize our complicity in this silencing. At the same time, she is empowering in the challenges she poses. Using her voice she speaks up, she speaks out for herself, for those who have spoken, and those who are yet to speak. Her campaign enabled voices to speak of a sexism and misogyny that had become so normalized that women were (and still are) disciplined into silence. She enabled the girls at the camp to reject this positioning. Indeed, the aim was to provide solidarity; comfort from isolation.

Tarana Burke's work followed a history of Black women's activism speaking out about male sexual violence towards women. Rosa Park's name is synonymous with the 1955 Montgomery bus boycott, often presented as the start of the Black civil rights movement. As Danielle McGuire notes, this was a carefully considered political act of defiance, but it was also the cumulation of years and years of sexual violence and exploitation of Black women. Sexual exploitation of Black women by white men is historically located in slavery and continued well into the 20th century.[3] When Recy Taylor was raped by six white men in 1944, it was Rosa Parks who was sent by her local NAACP (National Association for the Advancement of Colored People) branch, to work and campaign to bring the rapists to justice.

This was in a context where Black women had persisted in giving their testimonies in letters to justice departments and in Black newspapers. As McGuire observes, 'decades before radical feminists in the women's movement urged rape survivors to "speak out", African-American women's public protests galvanized local, national and even international outrage'.[4] Yet, at the same time, she argues, the testimonies of these women, their lives and experiences, the systematic exploitation and violence they were subjected to, had largely been written out of, and silenced within, histories of the civil rights movement. So when #MeToo started trending, the irony of the appropriation of Black activism by white celebrities, which served to speak primarily for white women's interests, was not lost.[5]

Mainstream media narratives reflected the ways in which social media became a powerful tool for predominantly white women to tell their stories and share experiences, initially about what was taking place in the media industry. We might ask, why did widespread sexual assault come as a surprise in our media discourse? If we had been taking women seriously in and through our media, we would have known that this was not anything new. Karen Boyle writes about the way in which it was an 'open secret' that women were harassed in the film industry[6] and about celebrity abusers who have been 'hiding in plain sight'.[7] But what social media did was provide a space where women could speak up and have a voice. It provided activists with the opportunities to connect, share, organize and protest.[8] The now global Hollaback! campaign started in 2005 with an aim to end harassment in public, online, or wherever it occurred.[9] Laura Bates's Everyday Sexism Project launched on 16 April 2012 and has increased in prominence to become a global phenomenon.[10] In these online fora women told everyday stories of the ways in which sexual abuse and harassment of women took place in those spaces that were not necessarily amenable to legislation or prosecution. Moreover, even when these experiences were classed as criminal offences women detailed on these sites how they had been afraid to speak up, as they felt unlikely to be believed.

Of course, it would be too simplistic to say that following #MeToo all women have been believed. The appointment of Brett Kavanaugh to the Supreme Court in the US, has been a notable case worthy of discussion. Christine Blasey Ford's powerful testimony was mocked and belittled by President Trump. As has been noted, it was interesting that Kavanaugh was able to perfectly document his war record, and yet the historic event that was in question was shrouded in mystery.[11] The questions that her testimony raised as to Kavanaugh's suitability for office, it would seem, were insufficient for him personally to have the integrity to stand down. Nor, notably, was this seen as serious enough to prevent his election. So what would it have taken for a testimony of sexual abuse to be taken seriously and to have consequences? Abuse of a man? Certainly, allegations of abuse of a man have been sufficient for Kevin Spacey to be removed from the Netflix series *House of Cards*. But allegations of the abuse of a woman are apparently insufficient grounds to prevent a lifelong election to the Supreme Court?

These men and #MeToo

What this speaks to is the way in which a particular type of entitled masculinized behaviour has become so normalized. It has become so taken for granted, unchallenged and 'common sense' that reactions are often positioned as something that are up for debate and discussion: how are men supposed to be able to interact with women? How can men now flirt without fear? These have been prominent in the ways in which the role of men in #MeToo has been positioned, rather than the more obvious questions being asked: why do some men do this? And what do we need to do for women to feel safe?

UK interviewer John Humphreys used his platform on the BBC Radio 4 *Today* programme to introduce discussions about the impossibility of men now being able to safely flirt with women, and wider media discourses adopted this 'poor men who no longer understand the rules of the game' narrative. During an interview about harassment in Westminster, he asked, "Is there a danger that we could go too far in the other direction and people will be afraid to ask somebody else out for the evening, or indeed ask them out for a proper date, maybe even eventually to marry them or something? There are risks in this aren't there?"[12] Yes. There are risks for women's safety, surely these are the only risks. When we do talk about men, surely the question is, why don't men understand the difference between intimidating, stalking, groping and flirting? It is men killing women that is the problem not women killing romance.

But it was not just men saying this; women were co-opted into the narrative that things had gone 'too far'. Interestingly, we were told that it had gone too far for the men who were being confused by the clear guidelines and messages being sent about unsolicited and unwanted behaviour. Astutely, for patriarchal interests to continue to thrive, women were positioned against other women. We saw headlines such as the 2018 *The Times* article '#MeToo shuts out men, says Keira Knightley'.[13] This article is reflective of a wider counter narrative, positioning women as defenders of men as a group, and their 'right to flirt' which seems to trump a woman's right to safety. At the same time, French feminists also gained widespread attention for their criticism of the #MeToo movement. Catherine Deneuve wrote a public letter which called attention to the ways in which #MeToo was being publicly discussed, lacking any nuance, positioning women as victims, reducing them to their bodies, and lacking any recognition of female freedom and agency. However, mainstream media reported this somewhat differently. We were told that the French feminists' concern was that #MeToo was about 'the hatred of men'.[14] The *New York Times* told us 'Catherine Deneuve and others denounce the #MeToo movement' (Safronova, 2018).[15] While the UK *Telegraph* ran with 'Catherine Deneuve signs letter denouncing #MeToo "witch hunt": "Men should be free to hit on women"'.[16] And while the *Telegraph* suggested that MeToo was nothing more than a witch hunt, what the letter actually said was:

> Just like in the good old witch–hunt days, what we are once again witnessing here is puritanism in the name of a so-called greater good, claiming to promote the liberation and protection of women, only to enslave them to a status of eternal victim and reduce them to defenseless preys of male chauvinist demons.[17]

So while the letter referred to a 'witch hunt' it was not a witch hunt by #MeToo per se, but a comment on the ways in which women were being constructed in public discourse as powerless subjects of men, rather than autonomous individuals in their own right.

The ways in which women were positioned as antagonistic towards each other, in and through these media contexts, failed to acknowledge the diversity of ways in which women, throughout feminist history, have disagreed on what emancipation and liberation for women looks like. The reductive positioning of all women as an homogenous group, also invites the further denigration of women as represented in the common derogatory trope of a female 'cat fight'. We might also note that in our media men disagree all the time, but this is not used as a mechanism to invalidate their argument.

This type of coverage was used as justification to devote discussion to, and reframe the narrative as, little more than 'how can we now flirt?' That this repositioning took place, and the notion that somehow this represents some form of debate around women's bodies, relies on assumptions of entitlement; men are assumed to be 'entitled' to flirt, entitled to catcall, to stop women and ask them for their numbers, to shout comments out of car windows. Women's experiences are delegitimized by expressions such as 'well you should think yourself lucky that you are seen as attractive'. But it is the erasure of women's consent in this process that is the problem; the unwelcome attention/intrusion into women's lives, which is informed by an assumption of entitlement. An entitlement over women's bodies and experiences which is highly problematic, and that has been culturally normalized. And while #MeToo has been heralded as a tool of emancipation for women, it is perhaps also worth noting, again, a slightly more complex media context than we are generally presented with. The act of posting on #MeToo is also fraught with hostility, especially when social media functions as a space where women are much more likely to be subjected to abuse. And this online abuse is increasing.[18] Women may be subjected to, and are far more likely to be subjected to, a whole host of death and rape threats.[19] In this sense, while social media provides a space where a diversity of women are empowered, at the same time, this still takes place in a wider patriarchal context in which the abuse of women is culturally and discursively legitimated. Misogyny, as Mantilla notes, has gone viral.[20] So how then do we disentangle these experiences and these contexts, in order to make sense of, and repoliticize, what is taking place? I argue that we can do this through use of the concept 'cultural sexism'.

Cultural sexism

To understand how and why sexism has become culturally embedded in and through our media, I develop the concept of 'cultural sexism'. Cultural sexism is essentially comprised of the ways in which sexism is both constituted by, and constitutive of, our Westernized capitalist culture. It functions through the silencing of women and the denial of their voice; through the disciplining of women into regimes and expectations of what a woman is expected to look like, how she is expected to behave, and her role within society; and through the penalties she pays for her public role, and the ways in which the patriarchal structure of the household serves to further reinforce the subordination of the woman. Cultural sexism functions through the assumption of an objective 'truth' that links wealth and masculine dominance, in the ideas that are promulgated in the name of neoliberal meritocracy. It functions through violence, both at the physical and the symbolic levels. And it is the interaction of these functions, that mutually reinforce each other, which is at the heart of the way in which cultural sexism is operationalized. Cultural sexism seeps through our culture, it undermines our legal structures. It means those structures 'fail'. Cultural sexism is in the intangible and unmeasurable, but like an elephant, we know it when we see it or experience it. It is a sexism ingrained within our Western cultural narratives, media content and engagement. And it is in this complexity of interaction that we become able to ask questions about the political nature of our social, political and economic structures. In asking who has power and how it works, we expose how inequalities become embedded, and within that, as suggested in the final chapter, we find an opportunity to repoliticize sexism and challenge and change those inequalities.

The politics of cultural sexism

Within feminism, we are taught that politics is not just something that is carried out by formal state actors and institutions; rather politics is about the exercise of power. And as soon as we recognize the relational nature of power we see that power relationships govern all areas of our lives, both in the public space (for example in media narratives, and in the workplace) but also in the private areas of life at home (in, for example, the relationship between husband and wife). Feminist theorists have long battled for the recognition that women's experience and knowledge enables us to make visible the ways in which power relationships affect all areas of life. Perhaps most famously, Carol Hanisch observed that 'the personal is the political'.[21] bell hooks, Audre Lorde and Kimberlé Crenshaw reminded us that the personal is not just gendered but raced.[22] Cynthia Enloe also connects the personal to the international.[23] This understanding of the intertwining of the personal with the political encapsulates two key components: first, there is power in expressing individual voices and experiences of oppression. Second, the cumulative effect and the collective expression of these voices can (and has) facilitated change. To ask political questions is to connect the personal and the political. That is, the personal enables us not just to see what happens to individuals. A focus on the personal enables us also to see those structures of power which legitimate and perpetuate these behaviours.

In June 2016, the US Equal Employment Opportunity Commission published a report seeking to understand harassment in the workplace. Women were given a voice to describe their experiences. While some women did come forward there were many who would not, preferring to 'avoid the harasser, deny or downplay the gravity of the situation, or attempt to ignore, forget, or endure the behaviour'. Why is it that women would behave in this way? Numerous studies have attempted to answer this question.[24] The focus has often been on the women themselves; that women feel ashamed, responsible for what has happened, they might minimize what has happened or be afraid of the consequences of speaking out. Women themselves may lack confidence in coming forward, or feel hopeless after seeing the ways other women have been treated or responded to. These of course are clearly legitimate reasons and concerns. But the issue at stake here, is *why* do women feel like this? To answer this question we need to look at the context that a diversity of women, and men, have their experiences shaped in. What is it that we are taught, that we learn, through our daily lives and experiences that mean that a diversity of women feel this way?

It is often the women who are blamed, women whose behaviour is shaped and re-shaped. Women who are expected to acquiesce, appease, and put up with unwanted intrusion and regulation of their lives. Historically, we see the rejection of patriarchal norms and expectations medicalized.[25] Women who did not conform to the demands of their husbands (or who maybe were suffering from premenstrual syndrome, period pain or the menopause) were diagnosed as hysterical. This medicalization of the imposed 'women's condition', much like our wider neoliberal narratives, focuses our attention on the need to 'fix the woman'. Actually, it is the system that needs fixing, not the women who reject its consequences.

There are crucial political questions to be asked about why it makes such a difference to your life experience if you are a white upper-class man, or a Black working-class woman? Why are (white male) politicians keen to dismiss these issues as identity politics? As something not necessarily worthy or deserving of discussion? In part, this dismissal of diverse interests stems from a blind spot. Because identity has always been at the heart of politics. The difference in our Westernized contexts is that political identity has been broadly white, heterosexual, entitled and male. But so normalized has this identity become, so taken for granted and so 'common sense' that differing interests have become dismissed as 'other', as deviant from the norm of serious politics, through their construction in derogatory terms as identity politics. All politics have identity. What the expression of differing voices and interests has done is expose that historically we have been given to understand that politics was identity free, when in essence it was only about one identity: that of the white, entitled man. The backlash emerges when different forms of identity politics are seeking expression and voice.

We are not witnessing a rise in identity politics, but a clash of identity politics. This clash of identity politics, as with feminist activism beforehand, represents an opportunity for a shift in cultural and societal values; an opportunity to repoliticize sexism and the structures that embed it within our society. Cultural sexism is both within our structures and belief systems, and operationalized through the silencing, disciplining and expressions of violence towards women.

In unpacking the ways in which cultural sexism operates, the term 'a diversity of women' is used to reflect the recognition that women have a range of experiences and interests, and that these may often be brought into tension within feminist debate. Exposing biological assumptions about gender differences enables us to see the ways in which the system works. Yet this exposure also functions to *obscure* the diversity of women's interests and experiences. To fight a system relies on collective action, and collective unity. But does this unity have to stem from biological difference? Debates around 'standpoint epistemology'[26] invite us to engage in questions of political positioning: can men fight for women's interests? Can white women fight for the interests of women of colour? Social justice arguments would advocate of course. But what then is the unifying category in which to fight the established (minority, entitled, white, heterosexual male) order where interests coalesce? These are important debates which reflect the embedded nature of raced and gendered power structures; who gets to speak, about what, in whose interests and how, are key political questions that underpin the repoliticizing of sexism.

Clearly, it is difficult in this current project to use the terms man and woman, given the problematic structures in which they are situated. However, at the same time, to not use the categories men and women might also serve to erase the structures that have been built on this basis. And so we have a double bind. If we talk about things in gender-neutral terms, we erase the gendered structures of oppression. If we talk about society in terms of biological sex, we make those structures visible, but at the same time reinforce them. My purpose in this book is to make sexist structures visible: and this is a political act. To make them visible is central to undoing them. Spivak's concept of strategic essentialism is useful here: we use essentialized terms so we are able to understand strategically how they operate.[27] And so I use the terms men and women, advisedly, but the terms masculinity and femininity to refer to biological and cultural positioning within a masculine structure of power.

Repoliticizing sexism, and asking questions about its cultural nature, means we must listen, understand, trust, believe, and support the women who are subject to these experiences. We need to make sure those voices are not just heard but listened to. Not only do we need to reflect on why this movement and moment in time was necessary, but what we can learn in order to prevent this happening again. We also need to ask, how is it possible that we have reached this point in the first place? And what do we do to prevent this happening again? We know that individual perpetrators have been removed, and yet they are also making attempts to come back. What is it about 'these' men, and their sense of entitlement, that makes them think that they have a right to inhabit that public space, while at the same time denying that space to women who do not perform for their sexual gratification? This sense of entitlement flows from an underlying structure that reflects the interests of elite, white, heterosexual, masculinity. And this structure is reinforced through the ways in which we perceive and engage with the world around us, primarily through the shaping of our cultural values and norms in and through media. Therefore, repoliticizing sexism, through its exposure, means we can examine the structures that we have in place, and how these structures set the context of our social norms, values and beliefs about the actual and expected roles of women (and men) in society today.

In the UK, we do have structures – legislation, organizational policies and codes of conduct – in place that are designed to protect women from violence and advance women's interests. Yet as noted in the previous chapter, they do not always function as we might expect: Laura Bates's Everyday Sexism Project reveals the horrendous levels of sexist micro aggressions that characterize women's lives; those which cannot necessarily be prosecuted, but are seen as normal kinds of behaviour, justified because of the gendering of our society. Our structures are being undermined when our cultural norms and values are in conflict with the aims of these structures. It would seem that, for some, it is still a normal assumption that a woman's body is there for the taking (or 'grabbing' as Donald Trump so ineloquently expressed).[28] In the 1980s Judge Pickles made headlines by declaring that rape victims were asking for it because of the way that they were dressed.[29] Wouldn't it be nice to think that those views were outdated? With echoes of Pickles comments, in 2018, a man was acquitted of rape as the defence lawyer directed the jury to assess what she was wearing, a thong, at the time of the attack.[30] To illustrate the absurdity of this, if we reverse the gender we might ask, how likely is it a judge would suggest a man was asking to be attacked because he was wearing boxer shorts?

The politics of sexism is embedded in the understanding of the way in which sexism is premised in a range of violent assumptions and underlying structures. But how then do we identify and articulate this violence? A 'continuum of violence' definition[31] suggests that the micro aggressions matter because they pave the way for, and normalize, the macro level aggressions to which women are also subjected. The everyday sexism that women, men and our media become inured to, and that women are subjected to, is not just something that can be shrugged off as 'banter'. We might suggest that if there was greater outrage at the micro aggressions, the perpetrators would have a clearer sense that any kind of assault, abuse or harassment of women was simply not acceptable. Men do not just suddenly rape, harass or assault women. This understanding of the interconnectivity between micro aggressions and larger scale violence towards women is important in making sense of how sexism is normalized, and lines of acceptability are presented as blurred. Kelley's definition also points us to the notion that there is not a hierarchy of violence for the subject of that violence. The same act may be experienced more or less violently by different victims or survivors depending on their own context. A continuum definition enables us to join the dots and see the interconnection between micro aggressions and full-scale sexual violence, while acknowledging that the impact of these effects may differ according to the ways in which they are experienced.

Conclusion

Making cultural contexts and assumptions visible means that we can bring a political dimension back to our understanding of the way in which sexism operates. These mediated processes of communicating our cultural values reinforce and normalize sexism and misogyny to the extent that we think that it is normal, or just do not see it. But just as the history of naming things, concepts, makes them visible, so we urgently need to talk about the ways in which our mediated culture normalizes sexism. If we want #MeToo to be a turning point, more than a 'wave within feminism', at a time when it is possible for things to become different and the landscape to truly shift, then we need to think about the ways in which we culturally normalize sexism.

MeToo/#MeToo shines a light on the way in which sexism and misogyny are deeply embedded in our mediated culture, both mainstream and online. By individualizing experience, our media and cultural narratives have served to move attention away from systems that perpetuate inequality and injustice, suggesting that the individuals who carry out such acts are 'rogue actors'. What this individualized and decontextualized framing fails to do is ask questions about the systems we live in themselves. We have an Equal Pay Act, and yet a recorded average gender pay gap of up to 20 per cent for over a quarter of UK employers.[32] In the UK, there is an Equal Opportunities Act but it is white men who are over represented in the corridors of power. Women have the right to vote, and yet our political structures are still dominated by white middle-class men. If we focus only on individual wrongdoers, we miss the structures that facilitate these inequalities (and more). So to ask questions about structures is to use MeToo/#MeToo as a route through which we can repoliticize sexism. Let's look at the structures in place and think about why they fail. Cultural sexism alerts us to the interactive and complex ways in which sexism and misogyny become embedded structurally and normalized in and through our mediated culture. As long as this happens, whatever laws and policies we pass, we will continue to see women exploited, oppressed, marginalized, silenced and abused, until we effect changes to this mediated culture that inform and shape how we both experience and think about the world around us.

Cynthia Enloe's work reminds us that we have to 'take women seriously' in our analysis.[33] It is once we talk about women and restore them to the discussion that we are able to see the ways in which society really works. MeToo/#MeToo enables us to reflect on what is actually happening to women in structures, but to ask the fundamental questions: why is this happening? In whose interests? And who benefits? To make these structures visible, we need an understanding of what they are. Once we see them we are able to repoliticize sexism. This repoliticization then becomes a component of collective voice and collective anger, with possibilities for creative and fundamental changes to the landscape.

2

Sexism

Imagine a society structured around eye colour, where those with brown eyes dominated those with blue. Or organized around height, where whether you were shorter or taller than 4 ft 10 in. determined how you lived your life. We do not live in this society, but we do live in one where skin colour and biological sex have been determinants of our social structure. But why? These relationships all rely on the interaction of exploitation and oppression, domination and subordination; clearly they are unhealthy for many within them and yet ...

MeToo/#MeToo has brought into sharp focus conversations about sexism; the very real sexism that affects women's (and men's) lives; the sexism that characterizes the society in which we live; and the sexism that is perceived as 'the natural order of things' in the way in which our society is organized. To repoliticize sexism, we need to understand it. So what do we mean when we talk about sexism? The term sexism suggests discrimination based upon sex. This implies a biological difference between men and women. This might suggest sexism is a gender-neutral category, in the sense that sexism can apply to both men and women because it is grounded in biological difference. However, sexism is not located solely in biological difference but the power structures that result from this difference. These are power structures premised on masculine dominance and feminine subordination, and in turn are referred to as patriarchy.

The term sexism can be used to define experiences within these structures which are underpinned by female subordination and male power. Sexism as experienced can be the source of great psychological distress.[1] Sexism as enacted strategy can also take the form of misogyny (a word that every woman needs to know how to spell!). Misogyny, interwoven with sexism, serves to reinforce this 'natural order' of a society constructed around the interests of the entitled, heterosexual, white male. In this chapter, I explore how the term sexism has come into being, the assumptions that underpin and have led to the construction of a society premised upon distinctions between men and women, and the ways in which this has become 'naturalized', established as a system of social order (patriarchy) and internalized. Once we make these distinctions visible, we can name them. In naming them we can expose the non-naturalness of these power structures. We can ask who wins and loses in this social ordering of society. In making visible these winners and losers, those who are advantaged and those whose exploitation underpins such advantage, we can challenge the taken-for-granted nature of these structures. Making these structures visible and asking political questions through the naming and identification process, much like the naming and identification process within the MeToo/#MeToo campaign, can make this sexism visible, enabling us to repoliticize these patriarchal power structures.

A brief history of the term 'sexism'

The first usage of the term 'sexism' was recorded by Pauline Leet in 1965. She gave a talk entitled 'Women and the undergraduate' at an all-male conservative college in the US.[2] Her talk was to a room full of male students, and she pointed out to them that their education had been designed to exclude both people of colour and their histories. Compounding this problem, she observed, was the fact that the only authors they had been taught were male, selected as they were by male tutors. Leet pointed to the gaps in their knowledge and the problematic, structural nature of this type of selection. She said to them:

> When you argue ... that since fewer women write good poetry this justifies their total exclusion, you are taking a position analogous to that of the racist – I might call you in this case a 'sexist' ... [In excluding

all people of colour and a diversity of women] both the racist and the sexist are acting as if all that has happened had never happened.[3]

As such, this silencing and eradication of experience, she argued, means that: 'the racist and the sexist … are making decisions and coming to conclusions about someone's value by referring to factors which are in both cases irrelevant.'[4] Leet points to the problematic nature of erasures of knowledge based on biological sex, both in terms of the decisions that are made about what to read, and by whom those decisions are made. In doing so she also gives us a vocabulary, a language, to name and identify a system, a structure, which excludes and silences women. A system and structure which relies on an assumption of masculine superiority.

The ways in which we talk about sexism has historically peaked and troughed. In 1998 the cover of *Time* magazine asked 'Is Feminism Dead?'.[5] This was part of a broader media narrative that suggested that women now 'had it all'; women were in the workplace, in higher education and in positions of power. There was no longer any need for feminism, the narrative said, and ergo there was no sexism. Of course, as Susan Faludi has amply demonstrated, this type of narrative was part of a wider 'backlash' against women.[6] As Faludi shows, rather than celebrating the gains and advances women had made, media discourses were focused on seeking to restore the assumed biological order of masculine authority and dominance. In this narrative of female success, media told us that women had achieved the equality for which they had fought.[7] By implication we are invited to understand that feminism as a movement and critical set of ideas is no longer necessary. If feminism is no longer necessary then, by extension, logic would dictate that sexism as a 'thing' would no longer exist.

At the end of the 20th century, Imelda Whelehan argued, we entered into a period where we were told that feminism was no longer necessary. It was nothing more than 'political correctness' gone mad. Men, it was argued, felt threated by the advances made by women, but in turn, rather than sexism being eradicated we entered into an era of 'retro sexism'.[8] In this 'post' feminist context, masculinity was reasserted and feminism was presented as irrelevant and no longer needed. What feminist theorizing and activism demonstrates is that rather than sexism being eradicated, systemic evolution accommodates the advances of feminism into patriarchal structures. Sexism has not gone away, it is just manifested in differing forms responding to differing contexts. The structure is still there, it has just adapted; sexism is multi-faceted and reinvented. As Angela McRobbie observes, what happened during the 1980s, 1990s and into the 21st century was that sexism was simply recast and reformulated.[9] Sexism was both taken into account (we knew that there was this thing called sexism) and then rejected as no longer relevant to our times and place, because we as a society had moved on from those anachronistic times. What this meant was, this became translated into the cultural understanding that we could make sexist comments and jokes in an 'ironic' manner, with a 'knowing smile'. Don't be offended (love), it's just banter.

And of course, once the experience of sexism is positioned as the problem of an individual woman, rather than a system, it is depoliticized. As Ros Gill has noted, neoliberalism as a dominant Western political ideology has further served to obscure power structures, through an emphasis on the individual and the 'choices' that they are free to make.[10] The language of emancipation means that women are encouraged to emphasize their sexuality as a means of empowerment. However, as Susan Douglas shows, this empowerment in our media narratives is only really available to young, thin, white, sexualized and sexually available women.[11] She illustrates how women are encouraged through these discourses to believe that what they really need to do is simply 'look hot' and 'go shopping'. This Douglas terms 'enlightened sexism'; we see sexism, we know it is sexist, but our awareness of it is used as a justification that actually, sexism is now okay. Allegedly.

The language of neoliberalism also obscures the ways in which women are encouraged to become complicit in sexist structures. If we are distracted (or depoliticized) from those structures, we have greater opportunity to buy into them and reinforce them. Alongside the insidious way in which internet pornography has become normalized in our everyday lives and societies, Kat Banyard details the rise of gentlemen's clubs on the high street, for which pole dancing clubs in universities provide ready-trained workers. She notes the increased production of playboy motifs and products, directly marketed at women.[12] In essence, she argues that capitalism has simply rebranded feminism and sold it back to us. Women are constructed in neoliberal discourses as empowered to buy into, literally and metaphorically, their own oppression. It seems that sexism sells.

One of the clever ways in which sexism operates is that it is not a one-size-fits-all category. We miss its multiple forms of expression, which we obscure if we focus only on the individual experience. Following her analysis of a court case brought by women of colour against a manufacturing plant in the US, legal scholar Kimberlé Crenshaw developed the term intersectionality to explain how women of colour were structurally positioned by multiple points of oppression.[13] In the legal case, the women argued that they were experiencing compound discrimination in the workplace. The court ruling found that these women did not have grounds for claims of discrimination, as women were employed by the company (the existence of white women in office work was deemed as no grounds for sex discrimination) and that people of colour were employed (men of colour were on the factory floor, thereby removing grounds for race discrimination to be proven). But of course what this missed was the intersection where these women were discriminated against because of the ways in which race and sex discrimination overlapped. The experience of sexism, as the history of feminism shows us, depends on your position within other political and economic structures. White middle-class women will be affected differently from women of colour who are also situated in structures which are premised upon assumptions of white privilege. As Patricia Hill Collins, bell hooks, Kimberlé Crenshaw and Reni Eddo-Lodge, among others, have argued, sexism is something that is also intersected by experiences of race and class.[14] Sexism is something that affects and impacts all women, but that experience is different depending on a woman's situation within other political and social structures.

Sexism, biology and patriarchy

'Sexism: a system for deciding whose confidence is warranted; whose is not. Sexism: a confidence system.'[15] Sara Ahmed's definition of sexism is insightful. In this definition she reminds us that sexism is a system, a structure, it is the very foundations of our society. But it is also political – decisions are contained in this sexist system for deciding who wins and who loses, whose voice is legitimate. To speak means that you have confidence, right? And you have confidence if your voice is legitimated. And you have confidence that your voice will be legitimated if it is heard (as discussed in Chapter 5). So a system of political decisions about whose views and interests are warranted, and can be denied, that is premised upon assumptions about biological sex, is indeed, highly problematic. On what grounds are these assumptions made, and how have these become structurally embedded?

Sexism is located in a biological assumption of masculine superiority, which is premised on female inferiority. It is a binary relationship of domination and subordination, located in the notion that men are biologically superior to women. This seemingly simple assumption, much like the assumption of white superiority, has given rise to a whole social system and structure that has become embedded in myriad ways globally. In the West, for example, myths that arise from Christianity reinforce this biological difference and encourage us to unquestioningly accept this domination; and so not only do we have structures of sexism premised upon biological difference but political and religious belief systems located in those assumptions too.

The ideas of biological difference as a mechanism for organizing society are also embodied in the term 'patriarchy'. Literally meaning the 'rule of the father' patriarchy works as a collective term which reflects multiple oppressions for a diversity of women, enforced by misogyny/misogynoir and experienced as sexism. The term patriarchy reflects the collective term for the underlying structures within our societies (historical and contemporary) which privilege men through the subordination of women. The idea that political and social systems should be structured around biological differences dates back to Aristotle, whose arguments about democracy were rested on the notion that society should be organized to reflect the public interest of men.[16] These writings about classical Greek democracy form the basis of Western liberal democracies today. The men in whose interests these public systems were constructed were also propertied men. Class divisions were established and slavery was justified. Public life was where affairs of society were discussed; women and slaves had no voice or rights in this public space.

The notion of biological difference which has characterized the history of Western thought has been used to justify women's exclusion from all areas of public life. This was based on the claim that men were rational (and therefore capable of holding public office and creating the rules of society) and women were emotional (and therefore not capable of being educated, as thinkers such as Rousseau argued).[17] Women's place was seen as being in the domestic sphere. Their reproductive capacities, for those who were writing the rules of society, meant that as child bearers, women were therefore assumed to be child carers. As the socially constructed norms dictated children be cared for in the home, the reproductive function of women was assumed to mean that they also bore responsibility for maintaining the home.[18] The dominance of men over women, in this view, represents a 'natural order of things' and a consequence of our biological make up, where women are simply a resource over which men compete in order to reproduce. In this view, political structures would need to be put in place to ensure that men retained the control over their lineage and this was reinforced by the emergence of capitalism.

In 1884 Engels used the term patriarchy to explain how women became subject to men through the economic structures of capitalism.[19] Historically, he showed how lineage had been through the mother; wealth and property had been passed through the mother and women and men had lived in cooperative and egalitarian societies. But the growth of property ownership within capitalism meant the men needed to retain their economic wealth, and they needed social and political structures to be able to do this. So, for Engels, women's oppression was not located in biological difference but a result of historical and social circumstance. This circumstance was then embedded within economic and then political structures (which were constructed to protect the economic structures). It was the generation of wealth that exacerbated and created difference and systems of exploitation based on sex, and in particular the development of capitalism.

Engels argued that men invented patriarchy to protect their own individual economic interests. He argued that capitalism and the acquisition of wealth meant that what happened in public life had to be protected in private life, at home. '[T]he man took command in the home also; the woman was degraded and reduced to servitude; she became a slave of his lust and a mere instrument for the production of children.'[20] Not only were women slaves of male desire but the system was further designed to ensure that wealth was passed through the male family line. As this became so, women (who were traditionally at home) needed to be kept in place. For Engels then, capitalism blurred the boundaries between public and private. The consolidation of capitalism and patriarchy necessary to support it resulted, Engels argued, in 'the world historical defeat of the female sex'.[21]

In her work, Shulamith Firestone adopted Marxist/Engels' methodology but rejected their acceptance of the 'natural divisions within capitalism based upon biology'.[22] She maintained that biology was extremely significant in understanding the basis of male domination, arguing that it was the biological division of labour in human reproduction which resulted in women's dependence upon men, and men's ultimate control over women. It was this biological relationship, she argued, that was the root cause of male domination (and capitalism, racism and imperialism). She was optimistic in her argument that technological conditions were in place that could facilitate the end of this domination. For Firestone, alternate forms of social organization were imaginable, possible and viable. Women (as well as children and men) did not need to be bound and isolated in and through the nuclear family. From this there would be no necessity for 'men's jobs' to support said family. Women (and men) could be freed from the structures of patriarchy through an alternate form of social organization, one that was not reliant upon control over women's reproductive function. She demonstrated that there is a profound difference between women as child bearers (a biological function) and women as child carers (a socially constructed function).

The issue of control of women's reproductive rights has long been of central concern for feminist writing. And while this kind of writing is often referred to as belonging to the 'second wave' of feminism, at the same time we can witness the relevance and urgency of understanding the consequences of this reductive thinking in relation to control over women's reproductive capacities. Following the shocking death of Savita Halappanavar in Ireland, resulting from the religiously informed legal denial to her of an abortion, activists organized vigils and campaigns, honouring her life, and demanding women's control over their own bodies. In May 2018 the Republic of Ireland voted overwhelming to overturn the ban on abortions.[23] Yet while women were reclaiming their rights in the Irish Republic, this repeal was hot on the heels of the removal of women's rights over their own bodies by Donald Trump, across the world and also in Alabama within the US. A widely shared picture depicted Donald Trump surrounded by six white men, signing a bill which removed US funding for overseas organizations that offer abortions.[24] The election of Kavanaugh to the US Supreme Court of Justice has also been received with widespread concern, not least because of the fear of repeal of the *Roe v. Wade* judgment (which enshrined in law women's right to control over their own reproductive functions).[25] The issue of reproduction is one that seems to exercise masculine expressions of the patriarchy excessively; somehow implying that it should be male-designed systems that maintain control of women and what their bodies are for (more on which in Chapter 6).

To build a whole society, an economic and political system, on a singular assumption seems almost bizarre. Consequently, theorists and activists have spent extensive time challenging this singular assumption of biological difference. In her work, which has been viewed as a cornerstone for challenging notions of anything inbuilt or inherently biological in the differences between men and women, Margaret Mead argued it was culture not biology that defined our gender.[26] That is, there was no actual evidence for the assumptions that men were superior to women (despite attempts biologically over the years to 'prove' this through measuring men's and women's brain sizes for example) but actually the differences between men and women (rationality versus emotion) were something that were assumed at birth but did not have any basis in scientific reality and were defined culturally. In redefining sex as gender, we can see how social and political systems, which are premised on biological differences between men and women, are not the products of inevitable natural facts but of social construction. In 1968, Kate Millett discussed how this social construction of gender ensured that patriarchy was not simply rooted in economic systems but was tied into our cultural lives.[27] Through her exploration of misogyny within literature she exposed the cultural underpinnings of patriarchy and demonstrated how culture functioned ideologically to dominate women and maintain their subordinate role within society. Patriarchy was not just seen as an economic or political structure, but a cultural one too, where misogynistic norms and values predominated and became normalized.

While Mead pointed to a system of social construction of gender, Judith Butler argued that there is nothing inherently natural about gender, but that it is something that is 'performed' on, in, and through the body.[28] Her argument is immensely powerful, as it suggests that bodies can also perform gender differently, rather than accepting what is inscribed upon them. Butler provides space to repoliticize the ways in which sexist structures position us in and through our bodies. Through this understanding we are also able to witness what takes place not just in our everyday lives, but how this performance is reinforced in and through our mediated cultural structures. This performativity of gender, while an opportunity to challenge existing patriarchal structures, also has much work to do however as sexism is maintained through misogyny.

Misogyny

The term misogyny is derived from the Greek *misein* (to hate) and *gyne* (woman). It refers to a more profoundly embedded notion of women's role in society. Kate Manne sees misogyny as 'the system that operates within a patriarchal social order to police and enforce women's subordination and to uphold male dominance'.[29] That is, misogyny is both a function and an expression of patriarchy. It is also specifically located in violence and hatred. Sexism is an interactive expression of this; the two are linked but while sexism is likely to follow from misogyny, you do not necessarily have to be misogynistic to be sexist, Manne argues.[30] The term 'misogynoir' was coined by Moya Bailey in 2010 to describe a particular brand of hatred directed at American Black women in popular culture.[31] This brings us back to an understanding that as with sexism, white women and women of colour will have differing experiences of the expressions of misogyny/misogynoir. But what this terminology also does is reinforce how the patriarchy is normalized, legitimated and obscured from our view (and thereby depoliticized).

Extreme examples of the expression of misogyny might be found in, for example, the recent Incel movement. The term was first used by a woman in 1993, known only as Alana, who found herself faced with 'involuntary celibacy' (incel for short).[32] Not without irony do we see this term, in its contemporary incarnation, being used in almost polar opposite ways. Incel as a term has now been appropriated by men's groups who blame women, and particular kinds of men, for their lack of access to sex with women.[33] Notwithstanding this assumption of entitlement to women's bodies, this expression of misogyny, underpinned by hatred, has spilled over into physical violence. In 2014 a man killed six people, wounding 14 others, in California; his online posts showed him raging at women for their failure to have sex with him.[34] In April 2018 a man ploughed into a crowd in Toronto, killing ten and wounding 15. His motivation was claimed as being part of the 'Incel Rebellion'.[35] As will be discussed in more detail in Chapter 7, misogyny and overt physical violence towards women has long been built into our social and cultural systems and structures.

But misogyny is not simply an overt expression of physical violence. Misogyny and sexism may also be communicated through the ways in which we are conditioned and, maybe unconsciously, express our policing of women. The internalization of misogyny can lead to the unconscious acceptance of sexist norms and mediated cultural messages which devalue women, and discipline them to accept their subordinate roles within society. These norms and values reinforced in media and cultural texts teach us that women's function is to be looked at and objectified.[36] Internalized misogyny also relies on the devaluing of women (her worth is in her appearance rather than her societal contribution or individual achievements), distrust of women and a gender bias that favours men. How many of us will look at a woman in the street and think 'she should not be wearing that' or 'what is she doing out on her own?' or 'who does she think she is?' While these may seem innocuous thoughts, the fact that we are much less likely to be holding those views about men that we observe perhaps speaks to the ways in which the regulation of women – about what they can and cannot look like, which reinforces the assumption that women's role is to be looked at and objectified – has become so ingrained culturally. Internalized misogyny is not only about assuming that women's appearance is what 'matters', but serves to reinforce assumptions about what a women's role is and should be in society.

Internalized misogyny is the involuntary acceptance by women of the sexism that circulates within our society.[37] These norms and values teach women that they are there to be looked at, objectified, that their value is in their body and their subordinate position within society. This passive acceptance and normalization of so called 'traditional' gender roles again serves to depoliticize sexism and misogyny, by hiding patriarchal structures from view. Sara Ahmed writes insightfully about the expectation that women are born to please.[38] She notes how this is manifested (and I would suggest an example of internalized misogyny) in the expectation that women should smile. The expectation that women should smile, and by extension, please, therefore plays a supporting role in the advancement of male ambitions. As she observes, men are not subject to the same expectation. This seemingly small insight is actually quite revelatory as to the ways in which we are unthinkingly socialized into our gendered roles (and the expectations of what a woman can and cannot do). If you are a woman reading this, next time you are the only woman in a room full of men, try not smiling, and witness its destabilizing effect.

Essentialism

To challenge sexism and misogyny is to challenge a social structure that has emerged from assumptions of biological binary inequality based on sex. There is a danger of course in talking about categories of men and women. As noted in the introduction, women in the history of feminist thought had problematically been assumed to be white and middle class. While some white feminists did highlight the need to recognize women of colour in their work,[39] it was authors such as Audre Lorde and bell hooks who gave those interests a voice through theorizing from their own experiences and wider histories.[40] Of course this raises questions about knowledge and the claims that we can make to it. Can we know what it is to experience racism if we are white? Can we know what it is to experience sexism if we are a man? Can we know what it is to experience raced sexism if we are not a woman of colour? Let us reflect on this in relation to two sides of the debate. Feminist epistemology and Black feminist theorizing has oftentimes been very clear that it is only possible to really speak of and understand interests if you start from that biological position which has translated into your social position of structural disadvantage in the current system.[41] However, while recognizing this, social justice arguments such as those advanced by bell hooks and Reni Eddo-Lodge,[42] remind us that while we may not necessarily have direct experience of race or sex disadvantage, that does not mean that we should not 'recognize our privilege'. This translates as, if we are in a position of structural advantage we are obligated in two ways: the first is to listen to those who are in a position of structural disadvantage and encourage them to speak. The second is that if they do not appear in the conversation then we have an obligation to ensure that those whose voices are not present have their interests spoken for.

What this means is that we can have healthy debates within feminism, but we need to recognize our structural positioning when we speak. It is clearly of concern that to erase the differences between women would mean that the interests of white, middle-class women may ultimately dominate. But to identify and discuss patriarchy does not, and should not, mean that we have to reinforce raced structures. Patriarchy reinvents itself dependent upon the interests that it is faced with. Its multiple capacity and multiple variations mean that we might want to think about patriarchy not as the patriarchy, but as patriarchies; like a seven-headed dragon where each head needs to be slain for it to be overcome and the multi-faceted forms of sexism it perpetuates challenged and repoliticized.

Conclusion

MeToo/#MeToo has given voice not only to celebrities but to a wider range of women and feminist activists who have used social media as a platform to speak up and challenge the abuse and harassment that flows from misogyny and sexism.[43] When we start to see sexism and misogyny/misogynoir for what they are, we make visible the ways in which the world works. This is a world historically located in notions of male superiority, structured economically and socially around the idea of patriarchal rule and domination, premised on biological assumptions about 'natural' differences between men and women, informed by biological difference. These assumptions have given rise to structures that are often invisible to us. But these structures take for granted that women's needs and interests are defined in opposition to those of men. In obscuring patriarchal structures, sexism and misogyny/misogynoir becomes depoliticized.

MeToo/#MeToo has also highlighted to us that we need to recognize what is happening to a diversity of women within our society. In listening to women's experiences we saw that the pattern that emerged was of the depoliticization of the structures of patriarchy. But this depoliticization also contains a binary opposite: repoliticization. Restoring the collective of women's voices, in all of their diversity, to discussion and to debate, means we can understand the systems in place that shape our world. The vocabulary of sexism, misogyny and patriarchy and indeed the notion of patriarchy as multiply configured, as patriarchies, enables us to see politicized systems of domination in operation. Exposing these structures through the hearing of women's voices enables us to understand how these systems are constructed along gendered lines, and how the assumptions of masculine superiority underpin this. In turn, this system of domination and subordination leads to a sense of entitlement about roles and places within society. In the neoliberal context, this sense of entitlement is informed by notions of merit. Who deserves to be heard and to speak, to have dominant roles in society, and indeed the fact that there is a need for dominant roles at all, is bound up with the ways in which we focus on individuals and their attributed worth within our social structures. The gendered expectations of what women are for in society are disseminated to us by densely complex media and political structures and so to undo the way sexism is ingrained within them we need to see how they function.

3

Media

Can we imagine a world without media? Over the years I have asked my students to spend time without engaging in any forms of media: TV, films, radio, social media and advertising. At first I suggested they do this for a week, which they struggled to do. I have incrementally reduced the amount of time I ask them to spend without media to the point that I ask them now only to try 24 hours. But this is still a real challenge for them to achieve. Indeed, the longest periods they have generally been able to manage have consisted of switching off a phone for a shift at work, and, crucially, not switching it back on during their break. But just try spending 24 hours switching off your phone. We are more intensely electronically connected than ever before. We can instantly locate our nearest and dearest. Law enforcement agencies can track and monitor everything that we say and everything that we send. Advertising agencies know our preferences and target us accordingly,[1] and as the Cambridge Analytica scandal has revealed, media, business and politicians have access to more targeted and detailed levels of personal information about us than ever before.[2] Media also provided the platform for women to speak out in #MeToo.

Media are not just technologies of communication, but systems of communicating values and beliefs. It is through media that we find out what is happening in the world. Media is where our social norms and values are shaped and reflected back to us. Media tell us who we are and who it is possible to be, as individuals and as a society. In essence, media is ubiquitous and whether we like it or not 'shapes the limits of our imagination'.[3] People construct meaning out of the world they interpret as they actively or passively engage with it.[4] The images and narratives that we read, hear and see, in and through our media, define how we think and talk. So in the context of MeToo/#MeToo we see a reflection of the ways in which gender is perceived and communicated in Western society. In repoliticizing sexism it is useful to think about the role of media; not only in how media present and represent to us images of women, but the ways in which media construct a sensibility. This sensibility positions the way we understand a woman's role in society, and how she is expected to behave.

Media matter

Media matter. Whether we like it or not, they situate us as audiences and citizens and frame how we make sense of the world. Moreover, if media did not matter, as a society businesses and politicians would not devote hundreds of thousands, if not millions, of pounds to advertising campaigns. Irrespective of directly provable media effects, politicians, business and media industries themselves *perceive* that media have an effect. For example *The Sun's* headline following the 1992 election declared 'It's the Sun wot won it' (having directed their readers not to vote Labour on election day).[5] Social media advertising has become extensively targeted to individual preferences, so that advertising correlates exactly with the users' interests.[6] The perception of effect is crucial in directing how elites and those who want our money, our votes, our brand loyalties, behave. Media matter because they tell us what 'matters'. Individually it may make little difference if we see an advert for one pair of shoes. But if we see repeated advertising for shoes, on billboards, on TV, in films, in our Facebook feeds, then we start to almost subconsciously think that shoes are important. Now of course, this is not to suggest that we are simply passive audiences with no critical capacity to discern the manipulation of advertising. Yet as McCombs and Shaw argue, media 'may not be able to tell us what to think directly, but they are stunningly successful in telling us what to think about'.[7] In this example, media are telling us that we need to think about shoes. But in thinking about shoes, our attention is focused there rather than elsewhere, for instance, on climate change or poverty. So we might say, okay, it is possible to think simultaneously about shoes and climate change. And indeed we have media environments that speak to numerous issues; advertising reinforces all of the things we are persuaded we need to buy; politicians circulate messages to gain our votes. But it is the parameters of that definition that are important; the things that we are directed to think about necessarily entail absence of other issues.

British history is a case in point. Our historical narratives reinforce very much a white, elite, establishment understanding of Britain. This narrative was evoked during the Brexit campaign with references to the Blitz spirit of the Second World War. Yet, what we miss in this narrative are the voices of the working class, as the absence of these voices means that we are encouraged not to think about them.[8] Women are also often absent from these narratives, as well as their role in creating the society that we have today, and the history of people of colour in creating the Britain that we see today is woefully missing. As Afua Hirsch notes, that we have a Black History Month denies the notion that Black history is part of British history in its entirety; Britain would not be the country it is today without the histories of slavery, imperialism and colonialism.[9] Our predominant narratives encourage us to overlook this; we are directed not to think about the raced dimensions of our social and political structures.

Media tell us what is and is not deemed important or newsworthy, both directly and cumulatively. The #MeToo campaign has received wide-ranging mainstream media coverage which has drawn attention to high-profile male sexual violence and abuse. Women themselves have been politically powerful in getting abuse and sexual harassment on to media agendas. And yet, as observed earlier, the abuse and violence that affected the women of colour that Tarana Burke drew attention to had not originally been part of what we were being told to think about. Our media are also not telling us, in our wider discourses, to think about the routinized violence that affects women's daily lives or gendered violence as a social problem; these are stories that regularly fail to become news.[10] Karen Ingala Smith established the 'Counting Dead Women' website in 2012, which details how, on average in the UK, one woman is killed by a man every 2.5 days.[11] But this is not a national scandal or presented to us as a national crisis. In the 12 months leading up to June 2019, there were 235 reported murders by knife. And it is knife crime on the streets which is the focus of the narrative.[12] Men are more likely to be knifed in the street, women at home. Media do not tell us to think about these levels of violence against women, and indeed it is implied by media, because of this relative silence in the news agenda, that routinized violence towards women is not worth thinking about at all.

If we are continually connected to media, we do need to stop and think about the norms and values which drive our media and shape our culture. This ubiquity of media means that we really need to ask urgent questions about the voices we hear and the interests we see represented. As Jenny Kitzinger argues, 'in spite and sometimes even because of ... audience engagement ... media can have a very powerful role in defining, maintaining, and even transforming the way we see the world'.[13] In so doing, media play a hugely significant role in shaping our world view, our sense of what is important, and how our society works (and should work). But this is not a neutral act. Media are often viewed as political actors, both in their relationship with democracy and the demands they face as businesses needing to make a profit.[14] But I argue they are also political in the ways in which they obscure the underlying structures of the world as we experience it. Real power is rendered invisible and we take for granted the ways in which the world operates according to race and gender.

I will adopt Cynthia Enloe's approach in which she urges us to ask, 'where are the women?'[15] Bringing women back into our analysis enables us to think about how and why women are present, and what happens to them when they are. It also means we can ask questions about their absence – what does it tell us when women do not appear? And when they do appear how are they positioned? To ask these political questions is to ask questions about the nature of power; who decides what we see in and through our media? To answer these questions, in this chapter I will look first at the over-representation of men in the production of media content; second at the ways in which women's voices are presented through the lens of political activism; and third at the ways in which media position us in relation to women in the legislative spheres of politics.

Women in media

Descriptively, in our current media industries, women are woefully under-represented and men hugely over-represented. According to a report published in 2017, out of over 900 Hollywood films only 5 were directed by a Black or Asian American woman.[16] This report also showed that in the top 100 films in 2016, only 34 had female leads or co-leads. Of those leads and co-leads only 3 of those female actors were from racially under-represented groups; 97 leads were white and 66 were white men. Only 8 of those female actors were over the age of 45 and women were 5 times more likely than men to be displaying nudity or in some form of sexualized dress. What this tells us cumulatively is that men have a wider platform for having their voices and variety of interests heard. Their over-representation means a smaller, less visible role for women. And the roles given to women serve to reinforce our understandings of the role of women in society. They are there to play the supporting roles in the interests of men, and their role is to be available to the 'male gaze'.[17]

In 1985 cartoonist Alison Bechdel, in her comic strip *Dykes to Watch Out For*, devised a test to highlight gender inequality in fiction. It is most well known for its application to films, although can equally be applied to literature, theatre and TV. To pass the Bechdel test the piece of fiction needs to contain three simple elements:

1. It has to have two women in it, who;
2. talk to each other about;
3. something besides a man.[18]

In 2018, only 33 per cent of Hollywood films had passed this test.[19]

Alongside the entertainment industry, we see that in news coverage women also remain both descriptively under-represented (in terms of numbers) and substantively under-represented (in terms of issues and interests that affect women).

The Global Media Monitoring Project (GMMP) is a collection of snapshots of news coverage from around the world. The data is collected by volunteers on a given day once every five years.[20] Their most recent data (2015) reveals a dramatic under-representation of women featuring in news stories: women are only 26 per cent of internet or tweeted news items; women also comprise only 24 per cent of people that are read about, heard or seen in TV, newspaper or radio news. This figure remains unchanged since 2010. This is highly problematic when media are framing for us what we should be thinking about, when as GMMP shows, 74 per cent of our online news and 76 per cent of mainstream media news is about men.

In the UK, Rupert Murdoch's Sky News and Lord Rothermere's Daily Mail Group own nearly 60 per cent of newspaper circulation.[21] Google's worldwide dominance (accounting for 96 per cent of mobile phone usage) earned it £42 billion in 2014, in contrast to the licence fee funded UK BBC income of £5.2 billion.[22] Google is owned by Alphabet Inc., the CEO of which is Larry Page and the president Sergey Brin (the founders of Google). Since 2014, male employees of Google have remained consistently at 69 per cent.[23] A Google 2018 report further detailed the breakdown of its US workforce: white women comprised 15.5 per cent; Asian women 12.5 per cent and Black women 1.2 per cent. Google's leadership now is comprised of 25.5 per cent women (however, their leadership data was not intersectional by race and gender).[24]

The reach of firms like Google is important not only in terms of providing platforms for our news coverage and media content, but it also provides us with cues as to how we should see the world. In the UK, 95 per cent of the population own mobile phones, and Google as a search engine is used on 96 per cent of those phones.[25] If we use the search term 'man' in Google images we are given options to see men in a variety of emotional, physical and work-related settings and we see the banner descriptors 'business', 'strong', 'thinking'. However, google the image for 'woman' and we see a focus almost entirely upon appearance and women's bodies, the descriptors 'beach', 'attractive', 'pretty' and 'cute' are along the banner headline. These images represent not just Google's algorithmic choices, but a series of choices made by (predominantly male) programmers.[26] This reflects a troubling narrative that does very little to challenge old fashioned stereotypes about what it is that women can and should be.

If media are directing us as to what matters in the world, then the silences in our media are crucial. The absent voices and interests in our media discourses reflect not an absence of a diversity of women in society, but the presence of interests of those who are predominantly white, middle class, and male. The presence of these white male elite interests and identities that are played out, articulated, and reinforced in and through our media are central to our understanding of what society looks like. Making this power structure visible through giving voice to alternate perspectives and interests is not just the province of MeToo/#MeToo, but has other historical precedents.

Media and women's political activism

MeToo/#MeToo is clearly not the first time that women have used media as a means to speak out for their rights. Mary Wollstonecraft wrote a powerful book, *A Vindication of the Rights of Woman*, as a means of communicating her argument that there was nothing 'naturally' inferior about women. She fundamentally challenged the notion of biological difference between men and women. Rather, women had simply been denied the education required to facilitate the prized notion of 'rationality' upon which men's votes were premised. She envisioned a full society premised on reason, one in which women were given the vote. This idea was seen as radical, attempts were made to undermine her based not on the quality of her argument, but because of her gender. Former Whig politician Horace Walpole publicly dismissed her as a 'hyena in petticoats'.[27] A posthumous publication by her husband who detailed her unconventional lifestyle caused considerable damage to her reputation, because she did not conform to conventional understandings of her gendered role.[28]

However, her work underpinned the rising middle-class movements in the 18th and 19th centuries which coalesced most notably in Britain in the form of the Suffragettes movement in the early 20th century.[29] Subjected to state violence (such as being imprisoned and force fed by authorities) the Suffragette movement fought for the enfranchisement of women. But the fight for women's enfranchisement was not just with the state. Media coverage reflected the fear of a threat to men's interests. In November 1910 the *Manchester Evening News* ran an item which read,

> it is high time for the men of England to wake up. Their most intimate interests, their most vital rights in civic life, are in issue. Is England to remain a virile land in virile hands, or is it to be made the appanage and the vassal of a false feminism? … All of this is involved in the plausible plea of "Votes for women".[30]

Yes, that's correct: newspaper coverage, the most prominent media at the time, were warning that votes for women could lead to challenges not only to the civil rights of men, but to their virility. And masculine virility here was presented as synonymous with the interests of the country.

Where women were visible in news coverage this was often as disruptors of the social order. Suffragettes were often presented as problematic and the cause of the problem. For example, on 18 November 1910, some 300 protestors marched to the Houses of Parliament. The levels of violence, some of it sexual, meted out by the police earned the name 'Black Friday' (and it is notable that this period of history has been written out in our contemporary consumerist celebration of Black Friday in the weeks preceding Christmas). However, the day following the violence suffered by the women protestors, the *Daily Mirror* ran with the front page headline 'Violent scenes at Westminster where many suffragettes were arrested while trying to force their way in to the House of Commons'.[31] The front page depicted a woman lying on the floor surrounded by police. This did not look like a straightforward arrest, this looked violent. And yet we were invited to read this headline sympathetically with the police trying to prevent women from 'forcing' their way in to have their voices heard. The sexual violence used against these women does not feature in this media narrative nor was the attempt by the government to cover up these levels of physical violence questioned.[32]

Susan Faludi's work points us to the ways in which media narratives have successively blamed feminism as the problem for the position women find themselves in.[33] Rather than exploring the structural problems for women, she exposes how media narratives have focused on the ways that women need to be 'fixed' to meet the requirements of the system. Moreover, it is not just women that need to change to fit the system, but the ideas that women hold about their own autonomy and rights are often presented to us as needing to be 'fixed'; feminism is often constructed as a 'dirty word'. As Deborah Orr observed in her commentary on media imagery and coverage, 'anti-feminist propaganda is widespread and still manages to characterise feminists as sex-starved, childless man-haters motivated by bitterness and envy of proper girls'.[34] She was writing in 2003. And yet at the same time, we see feminist activists and scholars who are seeking to 'reclaim the f word' and who argue that feminists should not need to keep reinventing the wheel every 50 years or so.[35] The generations may change, but recognizing the evolution of patriarchies does not render the advances of feminists before us redundant. Vitriol and resistance to feminist ideals and the advancement of women's rights are not new phenomena, and yet we see a continuation of mainstream media narratives where women's rights and issues are rejected and contested.[36] Or else feminist ideals are sold back to us as illusory post-feminist freedoms.[37]

As Emma Goldman astutely observed, at the time of emergent enfranchisement the system did not necessarily change in women's favour once they were granted the right to vote.[38] Changing the political system required more than achieving the right to vote. The suffrage movement knew this and alongside fighting for the vote, also battled for equality in legislation, equal pay and equal rights. These battles with political structures form the backbone of feminist activism. But there are battles to be had not just with the formal legal and political structures in our society. How we talk about women, and women's interests in our media matter. Negativity towards women's political rights and interests was not confined to the suffragette era. As women gained other forms of political rights, patriarchal media discourses found alternate routes to problematize the role of women.

Media and politics

Nancy Astor was the first female MP elected who took her seat in the House in 1919.[39] But a feature in the *London Evening Day* tells us very clearly that 'she got there with [her husband's] help and his bidding'.[40] From these first elections until the 1980s, women had never comprised more than 5 per cent of MPs elected to Westminster. 1997 saw the biggest increase in elected female politicians when the proportion rose to 18 per cent with the election of 120 women to Parliament.[41] In 1997, following the election of Tony Blair to office and the highest number of female MPs elected, Mo Mowlam coined the phrase 'Blair's Babes' to signal that women had arrived in politics (when 101 of the 120 women elected were Labour MPs).[42] But it is not Mowlam's powerful assertive usage of the term which our media ran with. *The Sun* ran with a headline, 'Blair's Babes', which positioned the women as adoring of Blair; this was not a one-off incident and the term stuck.[43] This was media positioning of women as 'other' and we see the repeated focus on women's attire and dress as part of a media narrative around politicians which serves to position women as 'other' to the male norm.

The notion of 'other' in respect of women was coined by Simone de Beauvoir, who opens her treatise on the constructed nature of womanhood with the phrase 'one is not born, but rather becomes, a woman'. The title of her book *The Second Sex*[44] highlighted how women are positioned as 'other' to the 'male as standard'; women are defined simply as everything a man is not. And this othering has a racialized dimension. Recent media coverage of Serena Williams depicting her as 'angry' fits within racialized tropes of 'the angry Black woman' and has demonstrated how troubled media are by the successes and achievements of a strong Black athletic woman.[45] And it is in notable contrast to the celebration of male anger that characterized coverage of tennis player John McEnroe (infamous for his outbursts on court), who in 2019 was quoted as saying 'I'm still the guy that's paid not to be calm'.[46] Spivak notes how women of colour are 'othered' by their positioning in raced and gendered structures. She argues that 'in the context of colonial production, the subaltern has no history and cannot speak, the subaltern as female is even more deeply in shadow'.[47] This is not to deny agency or the possibility of agency to women, but to highlight the very taken-for-grantedness of whiteness and masculinity as the standards by which all else are judged (I will return to this ideological assumption of the 'objective' standards of the ways in which we judge the 'normal' standard in the following chapter).

We have a media context which, while historically hostile to the advancement of women's interests, has evolved into more subtle forms of restating gendered norms. In a media landscape dominated by masculine ideals and assumptions, female politicians and activists become identified as 'other' from the norm. We see the usage of the term 'female MP' or 'female prime minster' or 'Black MP', to denote otherness and difference from the 'norm' of MP or prime minister, who are assumed to be white and male. The 2017 election returned only 4 per cent of MPs as women of colour (26 out of 650). Following the election of 10 women of colour in 2010, the UK press celebrated 'diversity' in the House of Commons. Yet, as Orlanda Ward has shown, what press coverage also did was frame these women broadly negatively and largely in terms of their race and gender.[48] This framing, of course, serves to obscure these women's political abilities or credentials.

Research has shown that (usually white) female politicians are far less likely to be quoted in news coverage and are far more likely to be positioned as wives or as mothers rather than as policy makers with political acumen.[49] News stories are twice as likely to be focused on a female politician's appearance, in contrast to her male counterpart; women are less likely to be reported and more likely to be covered negatively than their male politician colleagues.[50] This matters, because as the founding editor of *USA Today* Nancy Woodhall observed, 'unless the media reports your contribution, your opinions – your existence – then for all perceptive purpose you do not exist'.[51] So if where you exist in public life is not about your political views but about your role as wife, mother, or fashion icon, this has profound implications for what we are positioned to imagine women can be and do politically.

It is not only the silencing of female politicians, or a focus on their childbearing capacity, that reinforces the cultural and political construction of the importance of women's gender in politics. This is further instantiated by the ways in which female politicians are positioned as subjects for objectification, and the 'male gaze'.[52] In 2014, following their appointment to cabinet posts, the *Daily Mail* chose to run a front page and double page spread which focused not on the political abilities of the recent appointees (as would be the 'norm' with male politicians) but as they were women, the focus was on their hair, bags, clothes and bodies. With the headline 'Downing Street Catwalk' the *Mail* discussed these pictures with a particular emphasis on Esther McVey's legs.[53] Despite the furore this headline caused, the *Daily Mail* continued its objectification of female politicians on 28 March 2017 with a headline image of Teresa May meeting Nicola Sturgeon in Glasgow over difficult Brexit talks, screaming 'Never mind Brexit, who won legs-it?'.[54] These levels of objectification of women as politicians simply are not transferred into the male sphere. We do not see UK politicians such as Phil Hammond referred to as 'male Chancellor of the Exchequer'. We cannot imagine a headline that suggested former PM David Cameron had undergone Botox treatment, or that explored whether former Health Secretary Jeremy Hunt had a 'six-pack', or the state of the Brexit party leader Nigel Farage's clothing. And yet, our media normalize coverage of politicians who are women, focusing our attention first on their gender, and concomitantly, on their appearance, while white male politicians' raced and gendered characteristics are obscured; this is the standard, the norm, it is not necessary to make it visible. All of which serves to emphasize the 'notion of women as out of place and unnatural in the political sphere'.[55]

The ways in which media discuss our elected politicians serves to reinforce gendered norms about what we value in our formal politics and what politics should be about. The language of politics is one of masculine values and strength, and the virility of male leaders is discussed and assumed. Terms such as 'war room' and 'battlegrounds' are used to describe the terrain where formal politics takes place.[56] In the leadership debates in advance of the 2015 election, supportive commentators also attributed masculine credentials to (former UK Independence Party Leader, and subsequently, at the time of writing, Brexit Party leader) Nigel Farage, who was represented as 'a superb natural debater, [who] was his ebullient, eloquent self. He was the only leader willing to talk in robust language about immigration ... while he made powerful attacks'.[57] His masculine strength was asserted through his ability to make 'powerful attacks'. This language of violence associated with masculinity is repeated not only in political talk, but in reportage of the ways in which political debate is represented. In 2019, Conservative ministers had been widely reported as wanting to murder Theresa May (who was then prime minister). Now whatever one may think about Theresa May, this is perhaps the first time in contemporary British history that ministers have openly talked about physically killing their leader. Tory MPs hide behind the shield of anonymity, calling for her to 'bring her own noose' to the next backbenchers meeting and that 'the moment is coming when the knife gets heated, stuck in her front and twisted. She'll be dead soon'.[58] That Tory MPs were openly making these comments in the press provoked backlash, but no internal inquiry.[59] In the context of the murder of MP Jo Cox, these kinds of comments are clearly unacceptable. And yet they also reflect the ways in which mediated misogyny and sexism have become a normal part of our political landscape.

This language of misogyny and violence has translated into the public sphere on social media. A recent report by Amnesty International showed that MP Diane Abbot was subjected to 45 per cent of all online abuse targeted at women MPs in the last election, and Black and Asian female MPs received 35 per cent more abusive tweets than their white colleagues.[60] The way that we talk about women publicly matters. Sexism and misogyny are part of a wider discourse that has been normalized and legitimated through ways in which media talk about and frame our understanding of what it means to be a 'woman'.

Conclusion

While MeToo/#MeToo is a space for speaking up and speaking back, we also need to get to the roots of the ways in which misogyny and sexism become normalized in our political and everyday lives. The way in which media talk to us about the world, what they see as important and why, matters. It matters because media discourse is political, and determines whose voice and interests get seen and heard, and whose remain absent, marginalized and silenced.

When we think about how women are represented in media and in politics we might begin by looking at where they are situated. But of course this descriptive representation tells us only about the numbers of women in these areas of public life. It implies a biological determinism, that women will represent women (as a biological group) and women's interests. There is a debate within the literature about the extent to which a 'critical mass' of women are needed, first of all, in order to ensure reasonable 'substantive' representation of women's interests.[61] This also allows for a discussion about the extent to which men are able to speak for women's interests, or white people to speak for the interests of people of colour. To simplify this as only an issue of descriptive representation, however, reduces this debate to an essentialism which ignores issues of social justice. It is not only women who speak for and represent other women. But the descriptive under-representation of women does have consequences for the under-representation of a diversity of women and their interests in media and politics, and in turn, in shaping our cultural values and norms.

Feminist activists and female political actors have not only had to battle a political system which has historically excluded their interests. They have also had to struggle against the ways in which dominant media narratives position them. Unpacking and contextualizing the politics of the embedding of sexism means making it visible. A key way to do this is to reflect on how we talk about women's roles in society. We need to ask where women are, and when we find them, what are their experiences, how are they spoken about, where are their voices and where and how are they absent? It perhaps logically follows that a system built on an assumption of male superiority may reflect that in its public discourse. But I would suggest that this discourse is not solely comprised of the material context of women in media industries, in state and legislative politics, and in the ways in which media construct them. This is also both a reflection of, and an interaction with, a wider set of ideas and ideational context about what 'matters'. What matters in our wider neoliberal ideational context in the West, is the capacity of the individual to achieve. The notion that there are structural barriers is ignored, and when we talk about women's roles, or women's worth, this is often framed in relation to ideas about meritocracy.

4

Merit

In 2019, a female friend, who is also a very well-established and highly regarded professor, was asked 'did you get this job on merit?' In 2008, I sat in a university forum, where the vice chancellor was asked why there were no women on the senior management team. He responded, with no sense of irony, "we did have a woman apply for a position *once*, but she wasn't good enough". Alongside the notion that one woman therefore stands for all women, is an assumption as to what counts as 'good enough'. But how exactly is this 'good enough' defined? How can we determine who is and is not good enough, by what criteria are they being measured? Who writes that definition? What do we mean by merit? These are fundamentally political questions: they invite us to think about whose interests are reflected in this definition, and by extension, what structures and interests are obscured. While the #MeToo campaign was concerned with the ways in which individual women were abused, assaulted and harassed, this chapter takes as its starting point the need to explore how violence towards women is legitimated through the ideas that are promulgated about what is valuable in our society and whose interests they represent.

The notion of what is 'good enough' suggests a commitment to some kind of objective ideal of value, or worth, or merit. Someone got the job, or their position in society, or in the media, because they were 'good enough' or had merit. What I want to suggest is that our current understanding of merit is intensely gendered. In its contemporary context the way in which the term merit has become taken for granted masks a series of sexist assumptions about what actually counts as meritorious. It is unlikely that we would hear the statement 'we did have a man apply for the job *once*, but he wasn't good enough'. We would also not expect to hear statements made in public about men's absence in boardrooms, such as 'all of the good men have already been snapped up' or 'there aren't that many men with the right credentials and depth of experience to sit on the board – the issues covered are extremely complex'. And yet, these statements (and others like them) were made about women when, in 2017, FTSE100 companies were asked about the lack of diversity in gender make up on their boards.[1]

The term meritocracy was first used by Michael Young in his novel *The Rise of the Meritocracy*.[2] This was a satire, an observation of irony, on just how the wealthy elite managed to structure education systems and corridors of power to maintain their standing. But the contemporary interpretation of the term is one that has been depoliticized from its satirical roots. As currently in use, the term meritocracy has become synonymous with opportunities for the 'best' in society to rise to the top. In this politically rosy view of the world, meritocracy is invoked as justification for choosing the 'best' person (for which, read 'white man') for the job, or as a means to blame the poor and a diversity of women for their own misfortune. This notion of merit implies an objectivity; a clear set of standards and criteria by which we can judge who is 'best', who is 'good enough' and indeed what 'good' looks like.

In this chapter, how objective merit has become intertwined with our neoliberal political assumptions of what counts as 'good enough' will be explored. A measurable consequence of this is the way in which merit in neoliberalism is framed as being about wealth creation and ownership. As will be argued, government discourses of austerity and the celebration of wealth creation are interlinked with assumptions about what counts as 'good enough' or meritorious. In this interlinkage, the discourse of neoliberal merit places emphasis on the individual as the author of their own success. In so doing, it will be argued, neoliberal merit is depoliticized, making the structural obstacles invisible. We therefore need to ask, who is defining merit? In whose interests are the game rules being written? At the macro level, I will argue that the discourse of merit serves to shore up and reinforce masculinized wealth. This is contingent upon feminized subordination, and at the micro level this can be seen in both the impact of austerity upon women and in what happens to them economically in the workplace. Exposing these assumptions helps restore the politics of sexism to the ideas we hold as to the value of women and men.

Objectivity: how do we decide objective criterion of merit?

The idea of merit, of being 'good enough' to deserve a job, a seat on the board, a pay rise, vast amounts of wealth, is often invoked as though it were some rational explanation with some objective content. Rationality has been broadly used to symbolize clarity, the existence of a singular objectivity; it assumes a universalizing truth that trumps all others. Through the history of ancient Greek thought and Enlightenment thinking, rationality has been upheld as the idealized standard. But crucially, it has always been positioned in contrast to its binary opposite, emotion.[3] So a rational decision involves objective, decisive, and clear thinking, whereas emotional decisions are conceived of as frivolous and subjective.

Rationality is also the fundamental guiding assumption of neoliberalism. Neoliberalism as a political doctrine was adopted in the UK in the 1980s and has become an almost unquestioned set of guiding principles of successive government's thinking and policies.[4] Neoliberalism, in essence grounded in the works of male authors Adam Smith, Milton Friedman and Friedrich von Hayek, is premised on two key assumptions: 1) that markets provide efficient solutions to societal (and political) problems because 2) individuals are 'rational' and will operate to maximize their own self-interest.[5] As a result of these two assumptions, neoliberalism promotes that if a competitive market is established, the 'best' (most efficient) outcomes will be achieved. We might argue that neoliberalism itself is a depoliticizing process, as it asks us to put aside any questions that we have about the ability of individuals to enter a marketplace. This might be illustrated, for example, by the fact that in theory anyone can enter the Ritz, but in reality, only those with the wealth can afford to engage with what takes place there. This reminds us that there are wealth inequalities that prevent individuals from entering assumed marketplaces. Crucially, there are also gendered structures at the heart of this political ideology. The assumed rationality is exhibited by 'rational man'. It is the rational *man*, neoliberalism assumes, who will pursue *his* own self-interest, thereby generating wealth. The rational man in the neoliberal context is unshackled by government constraints, rational in the pursuit of his self-interest, competitive, and by extension aggressive in this pursuit.[6]

Aggressive neoliberal agendas have been pursued in often violent attempts to open up markets across the globe.[7] In Western democracies, where violence against a Western democracy's own peoples is not so much of a political option, alternate 'softer' ideological political mechanisms are employed: 'this wealth and lifestyle could be yours if you only put your mind to it'. Resilience and individualism are the ways in which insecurity can be managed in this neoliberal context.[8] In this myth, if you do not succeed, then the failure is through your own doing. The implication of which is that the poor are individually responsible for their own position while the state need do nothing to support them, indeed the personal responsibility mantra becomes a mechanism through which welfare states can be 'rolled back' and individuals can take 'personal responsibility' for their circumstances, absolving the state of the obligation to provide basic levels of welfare for its citizens. The history of presenting the poor as deserving and undeserving feeds into our ideas about merit where welfare recipients are regularly referred to as 'benefits scroungers'.[9] This encourages us to view the economically poorest in our society in meritorious terms. Which of course misses the large swathes of workers who are on low pay. The Fawcett Society estimates that in the UK benefits make up an average of 20 per cent of a woman's income, compared to 10 per cent of a man's. In 2017 the Living Wage Foundation reported that 62 per cent of people working for less than a real Living Wage are women, and that one third of all working women in the UK do not earn a real Living Wage that they can live on. Feminine interests are 'symbolically annihilated' in the interests of rational economic masculinity.[11]

Masculinized wealth

Notwithstanding the completely missed irony of Young's novel (and for further discussion and critique see Jo Littler),[12] the term meritocracy has been popularized in the last three decades as a neoliberal aspirational ideal. In the mid-1990s the then UK prime minister, Tony Blair, began to talk of a vision of a meritocratic society. In April 1997 Blair said, 'I want a society based on meritocracy'; in January 1999, 'the old establishment is being replaced by a new, larger, more meritocratic middle class'.[13] Blair's New Labour turned meritocracy into a symbol of objective positive value. This was also electorally astute: for who would say that they disagreed with the claim that the best should be rewarded? The notion of meritocracy however, in popular discourse, underpins the neoliberal (mis)conception that if you do your best you will be socially mobile, able to move from 'rags to riches' and pursue the British equivalent of the American Dream. Individuals have succeeded through their own hard work and effort. Of course, all of this may be true if there is a level playing field.

In *The Spirit Level* Wilkinson and Pickett show us that the gaps between rich and poor are widening.[14] And they are not alone. A range of reports and books detail the increase in the gap between the richest and poorest in our society and have noted the increased transfer of wealth from the poorer in society to the richer.[15] Films such as *The Wolf of Wall Street* reinforce the notion associated with the heroic creator of wealth (premised overtly in misogyny), and return the 1980s notion that 'greed is good'. In true neoliberal vein, spin doctor Peter Mandelson, in a bid to demonstrate New Labour's ideological commitment to neoliberalism, claimed that he was 'intensely relaxed' about people getting 'filthy rich'.[16] But this is not all people getting filthy rich. This is some *men* getting filthy rich. This happens through an ideological position that obscures gendered and raced power structures, and focuses on the ideals and interests of an individual 'rational man'. In the UK, the annually published *Sunday Times Rich List*, shows us who holds wealth in the UK.[17] And we see that wealth is male. Table 4.1 shows us that men dominate as wealth holders, being 86 per cent of the total top ten holders of wealth since 2010. Now has this really happened because women simply are not good enough, or is there something else going on?

Table 4.1: The Sunday Times top ten wealth holders in the UK by sex 2010–17

Sunday Times annual Rich List	No of men	No of women	No 1 on the list
2010	13	2	Lakshmi Mittal (M)
2011	14	2	Lakshmi Mittal (M)
2012	12	2	Lakshmi Mittal (M)
2013	12	2	Alisher Usmanov (M)
2014	12	1	Sri and Gopi Hinduja (M)
2015	14	2	Leonard Blavatnik (M)
2016	13	2	David and Simon Reuben (M)
2017	13	2	Sri and Gopi Hinduja (M)

Source: *The Sunday Times* published 'Rich Lists'

To think about the ways in which the celebration of wealth is masculinized, it is useful not only to consider this in the structural context of neoliberalism and its underlying assumptions, but also in the way this translates into practice. Following the Western 2007/8 masculinized financial crisis,[18] a stated aim of the then chancellor, George Osborne's, economic policy was to introduce measures that 'support a strong enterprise led recovery' which Osborne argued 'must have its foundations in the private sector'.[19] This was born from a desire to support the wealth creators with tax breaks and advantages. Government's endorsement of the benefits of business in pursuit of economic policy was accompanied by not only descriptive reinforcement of men's interests but substantive affirmation too. In business boardrooms, we see a dramatic over-representation of men. Noticeably, in the UK, in 2018 not only were 94.5 per cent of CEOs male, but there were more CEOs called John than there were women CEOs.[20] This being despite the overwhelming evidence which cites improved business performance where boards have a greater diversity of representation.[21] A 2018 Credit

Suisse report showed that the numbers of super wealthy are growing, and their wealth is increasing far faster than that of the general population: 0.8 per cent of adults own 44.8 per cent of global wealth. Men are still disproportionately the wealth owners; in 2018 the Forbes rich list counted 2,208 billionaires. And only 244 of those were women.[22] While some men are benefitting disproportionately from all of this wealth, women are bearing the costs of these rational masculinized neoliberal policies.

Feminized austerity

Alongside this masculinized wealth creation, we see a feminization of poverty. Combining job losses in the public sector (where more women are employed) and reducing the income support that the state was providing, means that the financial burden falls disproportionately on women.[23] Since 2010, 86 per cent of the burden of austerity has fallen on women. It is noticeable that Asian women are in the poorest 33 per cent of households being the worst affected. The Women's Budget Group reports show that by 2020 only 14 per cent of the burden will have fallen on men, and as percentages of net annual income per annum, women in the first and second poorest households are losing 6.8 and 7.4 per cent of their annual income respectively.[24] At the same time, as noted previously, men in the wealthiest 10 per cent are dominating rich lists.

Not only has the cost of austerity been passed to women in terms of job cuts and increases in caring responsibilities, but direct physical violence has been reinforced by the reduction in funding to services where women are reliant on the state for protection from sexual violence. For some time funding for services such as rape crisis centres has been devolved to local governments, and now we see the direct effects of this approach to 'slashing public sector' services: repeated closures of rape crisis centres have seen waiting lists extended in some areas from 3 to 14 months;[25] one London council's funding for domestic violence services had been cut by 75 per cent and yet demand exceeds supply by 300 per cent.[26] This denial of state income support increases vulnerability of women, with the further risk of exposing them to violence as women are often being returned to the very violence they are seeking to escape.[27] In the language of neoliberalism however, these measures facilitate these unequal (and potentially physically violent) outcomes, in the language of rationality which obscures the gendered structures of power.

The 'everydayness' of this gendered process has resulted in what Abramovitz terms the 'feminization of austerity'.[28] According to the Trades Union Congress (TUC), policies pursued under the austerity agenda have resulted in rising levels of female unemployment; public service sector cuts, which hit women's employment particularly hard; and increasing numbers of precarious employment contracts for women.[29] From 2010, the Government Equalities Office, which funded the Women's National Commission and the Equality and Human Rights Commission had year on year decreases in its budget so that it received 38 per cent less in 2014–15 than 2010.[30]

The rational linguistic choices used to describe austerity measures, from the left and the right, have incorporated usage of violent imagery and language. This language of violence invites us to be reminded that austerity is in itself a policy of violence, and this is more than mundane and routinized.[31] And while the language of violence has been used to describe and define austerity measures, what is striking is that this language of violence refers to those who are most vulnerable to this violence. The language of violence used to discursively construct austerity reinforces the notion that women are subjected to violence; normalizing rather than challenging this gendered structural positioning. The word slash has been a regular feature of political discourse in relation to austerity. The term slash is defined in the Oxford English Dictionary as 'cut with a wide, sweeping movement, typically using a knife or sword'. Using a weapon to impose cuts clearly connotes the language of violence. But, we are perhaps also used to seeing headlines which refer to women being slashed, the active recipients of violence. For example, on 24 July 2018 the *Daily Express* ran with the headline 'Woman, 20, has throat slashed in hotel horror'.[32] In this headline the agency of the male perpetrator is rendered invisible (see Karen Boyle for further work in this area).[33] But this also serves to reinforce the idea that it is *women* who are slashed. (Think of the genre of Horror films referred to as 'slasher' movies, whose *raison d'etre* is to show the slashing of women.) In the public sector, where female workers are predominantly employed, their jobs are under threat, and we see the language of violence reinforced in supporting the need to 'slash the welfare bill'.[34] In 2009, *The Sunday Times* reported the need to 'Slash public services, don't snip at the edges'.[35] Women also tend to be hurt most when public services are squeezed, in part as they make up a larger portion of the workforce. In relation to the slashing of wage bills we see reports that public sector employers are 'taking a faster and bloodier route to chopping wage bills'.[36] Alongside women's employment becoming increasingly precarious, the services that the public sector provides are also subject to the same kind of approach. Cuts in social care provision also mean that the burden falls mainly on women as they are the ones who disproportionately undertake 'unpaid labour' in the form of caring responsibilities, for children, the sick and elderly.[37] The language of violence, for policies which disproportionately impact women, serves to discursively normalize women as subjects of violence.

If we rewrote the story around austerity and wealth creation to introduce gender into our narratives, we might start to see how the neoliberalism and associated objectivity, rationality, are both embedded and obscured. We need to refer explicitly to the *neoliberal masculinization* of wealth creation. If we reconsider in gendered terms how our economic policies are discursively constructed, we might talk not of George Osborne's 'enterprise led recovery' but of a '*male* enterprise led recovery'. Taking gendered realities into account and re-framing Osborne's original austerity speech tells us that he is arguing 'economic recovery must have its roots in the *male* private sector'. Moreover, if we gender the phrase 'strong and stable economy' (where strength is already a marker of masculinity) we see how 'a strong and stable economy' is deemed necessary to create *male* wealth.

Gender pay gap

Intertwined with issues of masculinized economic wealth and feminized austerity, we also see that gender pay gaps and the way we think and talk about them provide further examples of neoliberalism and sexism becoming mutually reinforced. The suffragettes did not only battle for the vote, but for wider issues of social, political and economic equality. Despite a history of fighting for equal pay, it was not until 1970 in the UK that the Equal Pay Act came into force. (While trade union history suggests an earlier union struggle and denies the role of the feminist movement in this, it was the women's Ford Machinists Strike of 1968 which is often attributed as the trigger for the introduction of this legislation.)[38] Despite this, a gender pay gap exists. While paying men and women unequally for the same job is illegal we nonetheless see meritorious justifications provided as to why men and women are differentially paid.

Under the headline 'Female BBC manager turns down job claiming man in same role was offered £12,000 more' *The Telegraph* reported that in May 2019 a man and a woman, on the same day, were offered the same post as deputy news editor at a public news organization.[39] The framing of this item as 'claiming' implies ambiguity on the part of the woman's statement and we are invited to read the article with a degree of scepticism towards her 'claim'. The article goes on to confirm the employer's acknowledgment that the man was offered a salary of £12,000 more than the woman. This is out of kilter with the Equal Pay Act. Both were offered the same job, on the same day. However, the framing of the article is around a justification for the differential on 'objective' grounds. In the article we are told that the woman who was offered the job reports she was told it was well deserved. But not only is this framing of the story patronizing, but it simultaneously invokes the language of 'merit' The justification given for her offer of unequal pay was that her male counterpart had 'worked above this level for several years' (a meritorious and objective argument).[40] His job, in remuneration and objective terms, was 'worth' more than hers, despite being the same job. This framing of the story masks a set of structural issues. First, as Carrie Gracie argues, if organizations really want to eradicate a gender pay gap, then transparency of pay is essential.[41] Not just after the fact, but at recruitment. So offering one salary, rather than not advertising a salary, or a salary within a set of parameters, means that everyone does get the opportunity to be paid the same. Offering the same job to a man and a woman on the same day requires only the same pay, rather than extensive justification which suggests either 1) the man has successfully negotiated where the woman has not, or 2) that the employer had already decided to pay the man more, full stop. Either way we are left in a position that exacerbates rather than reduces economic inequalities, on the grounds of merit.

The UK government has recently introduced a regulatory structure where companies and public sector organizations have to submit data on their gender pay gaps. The data to date shows that the gender pay gap in the UK has reduced from around 45 per cent in the 1970s to 18.4 per cent for full time workers in 2018, and 13.4 per cent for part time workers.[42] The *Financial Times* tells us that despite the introduction of gender pay gap reporting '[t]here are still no sectors in the UK economy where women are paid the same as men'.[43] And while analysts scratch their heads and assess a range of reasons and problems and arguments why the gender pay gap still exists, the focus is usually on the woman herself (if we recall, neoliberal solutions tell us we need to focus on the individual).

We are invited to read this narrative as a truism; that it is the 'woman' that needs fixing, rather than the system. Women are inflexible, problematic, rather than the environment and structures that they live and work in. We often hear invoked reasons for women's lack of progression in organizations, or their under payment for the same jobs, such as 'well she was on maternity leave, which took her out of the job market'. And this kind of account is underpinned by an assumption: that it is the woman's choice to leave the job market. But this is only a problem because of the current structure of the job market. Imagine a job market where women continue to be paid their wage throughout maternity leave. And career progression was not stalled while women were giving birth to the next generation of the workforce. If opportunities for promotion were embedded into maternity pay, leave and conditions, then we would not be penalizing women for their reproductive capacities (which, let's be fair, the continuation of humanity relies upon). Women, after all, are the people who are providing the next generation of employees, and yet interestingly we do not see this kind of depiction in films, TV shows and wider media coverage. In a neoliberal meritocracy 'worth' and 'value' are often determined by pay and/or direct workplace experience; which in itself removes from the picture the structures which disadvantage a diversity of women. And so 'the best person for the job' and the one who 'deserves' the higher salary is one who is defined in terms of structures which benefit those who are in the likeness of those who created them.

Targets and quotas

Women are not only under-represented in economic terms, as bearers of social costs and responsibilities. They are under-represented in the upper echelons of power, in Parliament, in business, in media industries and cultural content. So how to tackle this? An argument regularly put forward is one for quotas. Quotas are very simple. They are a fixed portion of something that a person or group is entitled to receive or contribute to. While trade quotas may be subject to intense political debate, they are nonetheless presented as political necessity as a means to protect 'our' interests. And yet this protection of interests does not, it seem, gain such public support when it comes to quotas based around gender. Our dominant narratives encourage us to stay away from conversations about quotas, which are positioned as negative, a thorny issue, disrespectful to men, and/or disrespectful to women.[44] Introduce a conversation about quotas and chances are it will end in a heated debate. But as Rainbow Murray observes, quotas are positioned as a problem because they are seen as quotas for women. The merit argument weighs heavily against women in this way. They got there because of quotas and targets, rather than because they were 'good enough' on merit.

Murray argues that we need to reframe the debate about quotas. Rather than talk about quotas for women, we need to be talking about quotas for men.[45] If we reframe this discussion as having quotas of no more than 50 per cent men on any senior board; no more than 50 per cent men in Parliament; no more than 50 per cent men in lead roles in films; an economic system that ensures that no more than 50 per cent of men own the wealth, and that no less than 50 per cent of men share the economic costs of austerity, then we expose a set of structures that are in place.

This re-framing would encourage us to look at our society and see that at present men are:

- 86% per cent of the top ten richest people in this country;
- 68% per cent of MPs;
- 67% per cent of local councillors;
- 60% per cent of senior civil service;
- 74% per cent of UK vice chancellors;
- 94% per cent of CEOs of FTSE 100 companies;
- 85% per cent of chairs of sport and governing bodies;
- 82% per cent of national newspaper editors;
- 84% per cent of British film directors;
- 83% per cent of Supreme Court judges;
- 88% per cent of High Court judges.[46]

At the same time, the public debate around quotas has struggled to gain much by way of acceptance, so ingrained is our notion of a criteria of objective merit being the only marker for the job. We often see media reports of 'tokenism' as illustrated by reaction to increasing the numbers of women in boardrooms.[47] The way in which this argument is presented implies that women are still not there in equal numbers, not because of any obstacles that might be in their way but because of some kind of objective assumption about merit. Of course, this completely obscures the inequality of the playing field. Moreover, it obscures who has written the rules of the game. Those who have written the game rules have written them to reflect their interests. To undo and challenge this we could, for example, write job descriptions that focus on cooperation rather than competitiveness; 'developing' rather than managing people, has been shown to be more appealing to women.[48]

The idea that women are not in these positions for meritorious reasons obscures the patriarchal structures which suggest that men are there because of some objective view of merit. And yet, how many mediocre men do we know in senior positions? And how long before we are able to see women achieve the same levels of mediocrity and success? In this objective view of merit there is also a tacit assumption that jobs are not just jobs, they are men's jobs. Not jobs for men and women; but men's jobs that women steal. The assumption that jobs somehow belong to men by default, is highly problematic and reinforces that sense of masculine entitlement in a system that is defined by and for men.

Conclusion

The #MeToo campaign exposed the ways in which women had been subjected to personal, physical and sexual violence. This chapter has explored how the assumption of masculinized entitlement is embedded in our neoliberal economic and political structures and neoliberal political ideology. Merit is invoked, implicitly often, as an objective standard. Women are measured in masculinized terms. If women are not 'good enough' then they do not get the job. If they do not get the job, it is more likely that men's interests will dominate decision-making processes. It is the men whose sense of entitlement inures them to structural inequalities, who are writing the 'rules of the game' which inform how we think about what counts as 'good enough'. As Dale Spender argues, these men 'can't (or won't) see that their definitions of merit, qualifications and experience are nothing more than rules that they have made up to protect their own positions'.[49]

The ways in which sexism is embedded in the way that we think about merit can be seen to have devastating economic effects, as well as to reinforce the gendering of these economic structures. We have seen the consequences both in terms of the gender pay gap, the feminization of austerity, and the masculinization of wealth creation. Merit and the sense of entitlement which accompanies it, are located in and informed by a neoliberal context which privileges the individual, and the market as a solution to social and political problems. Structures are obscured and acting collectively clearly is not in the interests of individual advancement. Assumptions of fairness or collegiate working are effectively ruled out in a context whereby individual achievements are to be attained through aggressive, competitive, objective, meritorious means.

It is not only neoliberal policies which have come to characterize our politics. Political and media discourses are couched in the taken-for-granted language of meritorious competition. While the 'best' in this particular construction rise to the top, sexism is further embedded. When we think about how we talk about wealth, and roles in boardrooms and public life, we need to make gender visible. As Rainbow Murray argues, let us talk about quotas for men, rather than quotas with the implication that they are only for women.[50] Let us identify boardroom directors as male and female, and refer to feminized austerity and masculinized wealth, so that we highlight the inequities and keep these structures visible. In so doing we can see how the politics of sexism is being sustained in and through the structures and ideas within Western neoliberal capitalist systems.

5

Silence

While I was writing this book an item appeared in the news: the BBC had sent a freedom of information (FOI) request to UK universities about the use of 'gagging orders', otherwise known as non-disclosure agreements (NDAs).[1] NDAs have been a subject of wider media coverage more recently, given that Harvey Weinstein allegedly used non-disclosure agreements to silence his victims and their usage is becoming more prevalent.[2] What the response to the BBC FOI request showed was that in the last two years, around £87 million had been spent on around 4,000 settlements across 96 UK universities. While the FOI was unable to show the exact nature of each incident, be that bullying, sexual harassment or sexual misconduct, what is clear is that NDAs are becoming an increasingly routine form of silencing women, and to determine who can and cannot speak within and about universities. More fundamentally, the sheer existence of NDAs also reminds us that some voices have value, and some are silenced in the interests of that voice which is seen as having value.

NDAs were originally used to stop the sharing of trade secrets, but instead, increasingly they are used, lawyers suggest, to keep serial offenders of misconduct in their jobs. Helena Kennedy demonstrates how we have a legal system designed around, and operating in, the interests of men, and the NDAs work no differently.[3] Women as victims are silenced and, as importantly, offenders remain in post (and this is becoming more prominent in the UK higher education sector).[4] So rather than protect 'trade secrets' NDAs are now functioning: 1) to silence the woman who has been subjected to abuse (and it is predominantly women who are subjected to this); and 2) to reinforce cultural 'norms', in other words, that it is okay to bully and sexually harass women. Sara Ahmed notes, 'to name the problem is to be positioned as the problem'.[5] It is the woman who is positioned as the problem as complainant, paid off and silenced, while male perpetrators (and predators) are protected by the signing of confidentiality agreements. The silencing of women in institutionalized sexual harassment is therefore becoming embedded as a structural form, and patriarchal structures are reinforced and strengthened rather than dismantled.

This is exactly the kind of behaviour and culture that #MeToo has sought to raise awareness of, and yet it persists. In many ways, this is how NDAs are functioning; the victim is removed from the situation and silenced. Silence surrounds the experience for all who have seen it. Structures are used to silence women and their experiences, which in turn send the cultural signal to other women that the structures do not work in their interests. In this silencing we sustain sexism and misogyny; we depoliticize sexism, normalize it and embed it culturally. This means that women are being silenced before they have spoken.

What MeToo/#MeToo and the history of feminist theorizing have achieved is the breaking of silences. To repoliticize the ways in which sexism is manifested, then, we also need to be asking questions about who gets to speak, whose voice is heard, and crucially, whose voices and interests are absent? In this way, we can expose whose voice is heard and has value in our public fora, our media and our cultural narratives. These political questions will be discussed in this chapter in relation to: the construction and marginalisation of women's voices and the ways in which cultural narratives shape our understandings as to what 'counts' as knowledge. Finally, I explore the ways in which political ideas of free speech have functioned to reify masculinized interests.

The politics of absence: silence and voice

To be silenced means to be denied a voice. Yet having a voice is seen as foundational to justice within liberal democracies. Having a voice in society is also regarded as a crucial feature fundamental to the legitimation of modern political systems and democracies.[6] Legitimating political systems requires that we are able to speak. But not only do we need to have a voice, we need to have the *capacity* to use that voice. Contemporary liberal democracies are premised on notions of the right to free speech (more on which later in the chapter) which suggest the structural and ideological valuing of 'voice'.[7] If a voice has value it will be heard. There is also an implicit assumption that if this voice is good enough, it will be heard (although see previous chapter for discussion of this problematique). So if these structures define voice as something that is of value, but only certain voices are constructed and positioned as 'good enough' to be heard, then this raises questions about the legitimacy of our political and social systems. Our political and social systems have long been legitimated through the privileging of white, alpha male, masculinized voices. And these have been structurally embedded through the ways in which these interests have been presented as reflective of all interests.

What MeToo/#MeToo reminded us of was the inordinate strength and political power of collective voice. Our political and media structures and systems do not operate separately and are intertwined with our everyday experiences of them (whether we like it or not). Nick Couldry offers a reflection on the notion of voice as value.[8] He suggests not only do we value voice per se, but we need to look at the frameworks within which voice is expressed. These frameworks are in our media structures; the place where we talk publicly about what we value in the world. They are also in the ways that we, as audiences, think about what our media can and should disseminate. In that sense, we could say that the media is absolutely intrinsically about voice as value, in that its *raison d'être* is to 'value' voice. So then the crucial political question becomes, whose voice has value? To paraphrase Orwell, it is clear that some voices are more equal than others.[9] So, for example, we might think of the ways in which people from public schools are over-represented in the corridors of power. Does this translate into the voices that are deemed to have value in our modern media environment?

An article in 2010 in *The Independent* observed: 'If Britain looked like its government, about four million adults would have gone to Eton, there would be no Black people, and for every one woman there would be six men.'[10] This means that the voices we hear from Parliament are predominantly those which reflect white, wealthy, masculinized interests. We need to ask how and why these particular voices become the ones that are given value. There is nothing natural or inevitable about white male voices being privileged and yet we are encouraged to accept these voices as common sense, a universalized conventional wisdom, rather than a point of view. Gramsci suggests that to understand how the process works, we need to understand the role of civil society, which 'is the marketplace of ideas, where intellectuals enter as "salesmen" [sic] of contending cultures. The intellectuals succeed in creating hegemony to the extent that they extend the world view of the rulers to the ruled, and thereby secure the "free" consent of the masses to the law and order of the land'.[11] What we are told here is that we give our consent without realizing we are doing this, as we just accept, as common sense, as 'normal', the ideas and beliefs of the ruling elites. But these voices and values and ideas do not just exist 'out there' somewhere in the world. They are reinforced to us, in and through our media. Our media decides whose voice has value, and also the binary opposite, whose voice does not have value and is therefore silenced.

Silencing women's knowledge

Our media, of course, are reflective of a wider historical and social narrative of the way in which women have been positioned across time. Mary Beard and Joanna Russ have both written eloquently on the ways in which women's contributions have been historically written out of cultural narratives, and the ways in which the objective criteria of value and worth is overwhelmingly male.[12] Not only has this been in the assessment of what 'counts' as knowledge, but in the active prevention of women's contribution being recognized. Jocelyn Bell Burnell discovered the first radio pulsars in 1967. The Nobel Prize for this work went to her male supervisor in 1974. The Nobel Prize for chemistry in 1944 for work on splitting the atom ignored physicist Lise Meitner's work, and was awarded to her male co-lead.[13] Indeed, so commonplace has the writing out of women's contributions to science become that it has its own unique term: the Matilda effect.[14] In music, Gustav Mahler forbade his wife, Alma Mahler, to write music, even though she was a composer before their marriage and helped with orchestration. Similarly, Fanny Mendelssohn also wrote music credited to her brother.[15] Joanna Russ offers a detailed account of the ways in which women's writing throughout the history of literature has been devalued ('she could not have written that') or denied through sole authorship, and written out of university reading lists and canons of that which 'counts as knowledge'.[16] In academe, women's contributions are also less likely to be valued or recognized leading not only to the over-representation of men in the profession but to women becoming isolated, lacking confidence in their own abilities and sense of 'place' in academe.[17] As Gerd Lerner observes,

> the denial to women of their history has reinforced their acceptance of the ideology of patriarchy and has undermined the individual woman's sense of self-worth. Men's version of history, legitimized as the 'universal truth' has presented women as marginal to civilization and as the victim of the historical process. To be so presented and to believe it is almost worse than being entirely forgotten.[18]

The writing of women out of history does more than normalize the universal truth of patriarchy, it also serves to not just silence women, but to create the assumption, the hegemonic normalization, that women should be silent.

This has also translated into the writing out women's needs in our physical environment. Caroline Criado Perez provides a detailed account of the ways in which women are rendered invisible through our physical societal infrastructure: from town planning that focuses on the needs of men and work rather than women and caring responsibilities, to car industries whose crash test dummies use the male body.[19] Anne C. McClain and Christina H. Koch were due to take part in the first all-female spacewalk. But this did not happen, as the NASA space suits had been designed around the male torso; only one suit was available in medium size, that they both needed.[20] Uniforms across the military and police forces are routinely designed and produced for the male body, causing huge discomfort and physical danger to the women who have to fit into these clothes.[21] It is literally physically asserted that these are not places for women. For Criado-Perez it is not just that physical systems are designed by and for men that is the issue but that we as a society have been conditioned to accept the 'universalizing truth' that man stands for all of humankind.

We also see this in our linguistic structures.[22] When women marry, they traditionally lose their own familial identity by adopting the identity of their husband. While increasing numbers of women choose not to do this, nonetheless the cultural norm is that the woman changes her identity to fit the male model. Mr does not change his identity, and indeed it would be a rare occurrence for Mr to adopt his wife's surname. Regimes of language have long been viewed as reinforcing understandings of gender. Dale Spender extensively details how language functions to reinforce sexism and gendered divisions.[23] Her work builds on research which has quantitatively assessed the extent to which women are systematically secondary in our language structures. For example, she notes how in the quantification of words we see women repeatedly referred to in negative terms, she notes how there are consistently more negative terms for women, without the semantic equivalent for men, and the ways in which women are marked as 'other', such as 'lady doctor', 'female judge', 'woman MP' and so on. This happens in professional and leisure spaces. 'Women's rugby' and 'rugby', rather than 'men's rugby' and 'women's rugby'. Football is 'women's football' and men's football is simply referred to as 'football'.[24] That is, male football is assumed to be the norm, the standard, and needs no identification. We are drawn to the aberration of women playing football, by marking it as such. If we retitled sports pages in our newspapers by gender, we would soon come to realize that we were talking about men's golf, men's boxing, men's cycling. This masculine assumption about the province of sport is reinforced through a quick Google image search. Through this quick search, we are shown that the default assumption of the term 'sports star' is indeed predominantly male. At the time of writing an image search returned 10 sports stars across the first two lines of images. Only one was female.

Notably not only are sports represented as majority male, but the top banner on this image page gave a separate option of 'woman'. This serves to reinforce the notion that female sport is somehow 'other' from actual real sport. This marking of women as other serves to reinforce and normalize the masculine 'norm'. As Spender argues, this functioning of language in gendered (she argues, sexist) terms means that the 'semantic derogation of women fulfils a dual function: it helps to construct female inferiority and it also helps confirm it'.[25]

Not only do we see this in the mediated formal politics of the state, but we see this in other professions. For example, the norm of the male in professional roles is emphasized in a quick Google image search for the term 'professor'. The top eight images returned, on a random day in 2019, depict men. The words in the banner headline read: 'math; physics; old; male'. The second image depicts a young boy; this also suggests to us that it is young boys who grow up to become professors (and by implication, not young girls).

This silencing of women in history and in our physical, linguistic and media structures becomes embodied in the ways in which we behave. These norms of women being silenced are linked not only to individual women themselves. The subjugation of women relies on a social system which is constructed upon perceived differences between men and women based on biological difference, which has been reinforced through the history of Western thought.[26] The silencing of women explicitly through the phenomenon now referred to as 'mansplaining' (attributed to the work of Rebecca Solnit)[27] or implicitly through reinforcing gendered power structures has an impact. Constructing our social and knowledge systems along this biological dualism is also evident in the ways that we think about how knowledge is constructed. Western thought located in mind/body dualism reinforces these biological differences where 'man is mind and represents culture: the rational, unified, thinking subject; woman is body and represents nature: irrational, emotional and driven by instinct and physical need'.[28] The rational thinking subject is of course consistent with the neoliberal individual; where women are biologically and epistemologically conceived of as emotional, this serves to negate, marginalize and silence their claims and contributions to knowledge.

Silencing women online

While women have successfully challenged their silencing of abuse through the #MeToo campaign, nonetheless social media is also a site where extensive silencing, particularly of women, takes place. Women are subjected to an increasing amount of online hostility.[29] Women are subjected to death threats and rape threats.[30] Trolling is a gendered phenomenon;[31] women are more likely to be trolled, men more likely to troll.[32] And women are experiencing online abuse in epidemic proportions.[33] The Pew Research Centre reports that over 70 per cent of women view online harassment as a major problem; 83 per cent of young women say that online harassment is not taken seriously enough, in contrast to 73 per cent of men who say it is taken *too* seriously and 46 per cent of men who do not see online harassment as a major problem.[34] These stark gendered differences in experiences and perceptions of the value of women's voice in online spaces, reinforce the notion that online spaces are 'white male playgrounds'.[35] Misogyny is networked.[36]

Media reinforce a gendered narrative of trolling by focusing attention on women as victims, rather than men as perpetrators.[37] A 2018 headline in *The Sun* ran 'HORRIBLE C★★★' woman, 26, trolled online after "brutal" video of her squashing enormous spider goes viral'.[38] In this framing we are initially perhaps encouraged to see the woman as a victim, but we are also invited to share the disgust of the trolls. The opening headline repeats the abuse she was subjected to, and the justification of this abuse forms the second part of the headline. We are also given screenshots of her undertaking this 'brutal' act. And yet what we are not invited to do is to ask why and how trolls think it is acceptable to respond like this to a woman posting online. Why are our wider media narratives not simply telling men not to troll in the first place? In these media discourses, invisibilizing the agency that male trolls enact ensures the narrative is structured around women. This framing by extension serves to implicate the responsibility that women have to protect themselves, rather than the responsibility that men have not to adopt this behaviour in the first place.

In 2017, Lola Olufemi was a Cambridge student who was subjected to vile trolling when she campaigned for more people of colour to be included on her reading list in an attempt to 'decolonize' the curriculum.[39] It is not without irony to note that this racist and misogynistic abuse increased following the way in which *The Telegraph* ran the story with the front page headline 'Student forces Cambridge to drop white authors'. While they subsequently printed a correction to the word 'forces', this was on page two.[40] By then the damage had been done. The student herself was positioned on the front page as the problem, cleverly obscuring the structures of racism which have seen people of colour marginalized in the curriculum. The way in which this issue was framed contains a further implied assumption of white male entitlement: that white authors should be there by default, and somehow women and people of colour need to 'earn' their place. There are limited spaces of knowledge, and these belong to white men, is the implication. These are the white masculinized interests who have successfully set the standards of what counts as meritorious.

In contrast, however, social media can also function politically as a way in which the dominant discourses that frame our mainstream media can be challenged, for example, the way that we are positioned by dominant narratives to think about police brutality in the murder of Black men. Trayvon Martin; his murder on 26 February 2012 became one of the most high profile media stories of the year according to the Pew Research Centre[41] following the release of the tapes of the phone calls where George Zimmerman (later acquitted of his murder) had been advised not to follow Martin, which really saw the explosion of simmering anger on social media.[42] In this sense, social media was able to repoliticize issues around racism. What we are taught by dominant media narratives is that when thinking about gendered and raced violence the former is something that happens to white women, the latter to Black men. Women of colour are erased in our discourses. And yet, women of colour are more likely to be unarmed than any other demographic when they are killed.[43] The coding of police brutality and violence as raced and gendered seems to reinforce a universal truth of Black male victims.

While it is clearly important to recognize these raced atrocities, we also need to restore women to this story too. The universalizing white masculine narrative cannot account for women of colour and in this way women of colour are subject to a double bind of mediated marginalization and silencing. In the period 2012–16, at least 20 women of colour were killed in police-related incidents in the US.[44] Natasha McKenna, Tanisha Anderson, Michelle Cusseaux, Aura Rosser, these are the names we do not necessarily know from our mainstream media but these are just some of the women who have died as a result of police brutality in the US; it has been the #SayHerName campaign that has sought to restore these women's voices and experiences to public attention.[45] Twitter has become a site where feminist activists have fought back against gendered and racialized abuse. It has been a particularly significant site for Black women, whose voices are often marginalized or silenced within mainstream media[46] and a range of feminist activists have mobilized solidarity and support for each other through social media platforms.[47]

Silence, free speech and violence

But that which happens online and in our mainstream media is underpinned by fierce debates around freedom of speech. All of what we give value to, when we speak, is located within a fundamental premise: that freedom of speech is a 'good thing'. Free speech arguments are often invoked, interestingly, by extreme right or misogynistic speakers. Liberal democracies are premised upon the ideal of free speech. Resistance of regulation of online media is often framed as an issue of protection of freedom of speech. Free speech, the right to have a voice, as noted previously, is a fundamental feature of Western societies. But it is worth thinking about what we are actually protecting when we protect this right to free speech. It seems we are protecting the right to have a voice; that a voice has value, and so the author of that voice has a right to express it, and by extension be heard. But this is in tension with a media environment where decisions are made as to who does and does not have the right to free speech.

The ideal of free speech is located in notions of freedom. The key thinker who has informed the evolution of our understanding of this is John Stuart Mill.[48] In his book *On Liberty* he writes that the only principle by which governments and states should intervene and restrict liberty is in order to prevent 'harm' to others.[49] But Mill does not define harm. This is left open to interpretation and is where we see sexist cultures and structures seep through and hegemonic masculinity structurally embedded. So how do we define the harm done to others? Jess Phillips MP has reported receiving 600 online rape threats in one night.[50] Diane Abbott was subjected to more abuse (which was primarily directed at her race and gender) at the last election than any other MP.[51] While women have been using social media to speak up and out, they also regularly have their right to free speech taken away from them in mediated contexts. This happens in the absence of women's voices and interests in media coverage, and is happening online when women are silenced through rape and death threats. Clearly harm is being done to these women and yet we still do not have misogyny as a criterion of hate speech in our legislative structures. It would seem that this kind of 'harm' is permissible irrespective of the damage it does to the receiver and the sexism and misogyny it perpetuates.

The defence of free speech is also located in liberal emphasis on the individual as the holder of rights and freedoms. And as the use of NDAs has shown us, this has structural effects in silencing women. Structural effects and consequences are missed if we focus only on the rights of the individual. If we only focus on individuals as having the right to freedom of speech, we miss the relational dimension; that having freedom to speak is a relational concept. This is related to a structural context, not just the listener. It is related to the underlying fraternity of patriarchy which, as noted previously, has structured our history. As Carole Pateman notes, the 'trick' has been to insist that fraternity is a universal phenomenon; a metaphor for a community.[52] The universal 'truth' however, as already noted, is a universal truth which reflects *men's* interests, not all interests. We see this enshrined in government, which determines the limits of our free speech, as 'the organs of government were designed by men, are operated by men, and continue to be controlled by men'.[53] The very rules of the game, and the parameters of permissibility, are established to advantage those who created the game.

The debate around free speech also suggests a sense of entitlement to have your voice heard. It suggests a relational component whereby you speak and you are heard, and therefore legitimated in your position in society, by the act of speaking, rather than the content of what is said. But if you are not able to speak in a mediated environment, the value of your voice and its legitimation are denied before you have even spoken. This writing out of women and women's experiences constitutes what Gayatri Spivak terms 'epistemic violence'.[54] That is, the violence is not physical but becomes endemic in the ways in which we determine what does and does not count as knowledge and experience. Violence is inflicted on marginalized groups and eliminates their contributions to knowledge. Spivak asked, 'can the subaltern speak?' and what she argued was that through the silencing of voice, the subaltern (the 'othered' group) is unable to be heard.[55] To have voice is to be listened to, and to be listened to requires attention (and respect) on the part of the listener. If you are not heard, you are not considered to have spoken, and if you have not spoken, debates about free speech become structurally unavailable to you. So the silencing of voice in this way creates a double bind, not only in the marginalization of a diversity of voices and interests from our understandings of norms and behaviours within a society, but also from the right to articulate those interests in the first place.

The ways in which the game is played out, and free speech is voiced and given value, is in our media.[56] As Nancy Fraser has noted though, this space for free speech and discussion (the public sphere) has been historically conceived and conceptualized as a male-dominated space that speaks to the interests of the wealthy.[57] Women's voices are structured out of and excluded from this space.[58] In mediatized discussions around free speech and attempts to prevent the regulation of the 'public sphere' there is often an implied if not overt assumption that sites where free speech occurs are gender blind. However, as Nancy Fraser identifies, gender blind does not mean gender neutral.[59] Indeed, the assumption that gender is not an issue, that women's interests are the same as men's, means that discussions which ignore the issue of gender serve to reinforce structural and cultural inequalities, rather than challenge them. If women's voices are to have value, then the ways in which the parameters of that voice is structured, by definition, must be taken into account.

Conclusion

Our social and political systems are premised on the notion that having a voice matters. However, the capacity to have and exercise voice in a meaningful way is manifested in gendered terms. The terrain of where and how we get to speak is not gender neutral. Masculinized experiences and perspectives about the world are assumed to conform to an objective standard. Women have historically been silenced in terms of not just their contributions to knowledge, but in the expectations of the roles that they play within society. The expectations of what these roles are and what they should look like have been defined in patriarchal interests. In 1892, in *The Yellow Wallpaper*, Charlotte Gilman Perkins fictionalized her observations of the ways in which women were subjected to silencing for their failure to conform to sexist conventions as to their role in society. Her protagonist narrated how she was subjected to 'silencing' through the medicalization of the expectations placed upon her within the patriarchal structures she was living in.[60] Shut in a room, to treat her depression (caused by the restrictive assumptions about what it was possible for her to be and do, and her refusal to conform to the male demands placed upon her), male doctors and her husband assumed that they knew, and made decisions about what was in her best interests; women were assumed to be too weak to know themselves and their own minds.

MeToo/#MeToo sees women exercising voice with powerful consequences. But the capacity to exercise voice and have that voice heard is not solely about technology. It is connected to a cultural environment where assumptions are made about who is entitled to have voice. When women are trolled and shouted down online, it can shut them up, prevent them speaking. When women's achievements are denied, ignored or marginalized, we do further violence to women in marginalizing their contributions. This silencing means that we miss out on opportunities to benefit from the contributions that women make to society. We also do violence to women in silencing them, and disciplining them into positions of silence when we make sexist assumptions about who exactly is entitled to speak, and we silence them before they can speak. Fundamental to breaking this silence, and refusing to be defined by it, is the importance of women speaking up and speaking out. As MeToo/#MeToo reminds us, using voice loudly, angrily and creatively, is a hugely powerful 'fuck you' means of rejecting sexism and our patriarchal positioning, which I return to as 'fuck this' in the final chapter.

6

Discipline

Can we imagine a man being told that his only function in society was to be a father, a husband and homemaker? That at all times he must be toned and 'beach body ready', and that this body must be available for continued touching, commentary and objectification? That he must see how our media lust after him when he is younger, desperate for him to be 'legal' but once he passes the age of 25 he would pretty much disappear from view? While this might sound vaguely ridiculous, this is of course the mirror of mediated cultural assumptions that are made about women. These assumptions, about the roles that women should and should not play, are located in the ways in which, both historically and contemporarily, women are 'disciplined' into social expectations. We see women's bodies being disciplined by our mainstream media as to what a woman is supposed to look like (young, thin, white and blonde) and what role she is supposed to play in public life (home maker, and if she tries to 'have it all' it will inevitably go wrong, she will only find happiness in a good man) and we see the cultural disciplining of women in micro, everyday cultural norms. If we want to understand how and why there has been a sense of entitlement from the men exposed by the #MeToo phenomenon, then it is useful to explore the context in which we construct and regulate women in our media, public and cultural spaces.

The disciplining of women is not only confined to their bodies and expectations of the roles that they should play within society, but their views and contributions have been silenced through history (as noted in the previous chapter). The objective value of worth, contained in the meritocracy myth further reinforces the way in which our gendered roles are experienced and understood. The value that we afford women's voices and worth is also reinforced through the ways in which we socialize, discipline and regulate women. These processes are often so subtle, indeed, seen as 'normal' hegemonic common sense, that we do not even notice that they are happening. They impact upon women's and men's perceptions of the world. The ways in which women's bodies are disciplined was highlighted through MeToo/#MeToo because in the stories that women told, we were reminded of the expectation of sexual availability of women, and a sense that some men seem to have, that they are entitled to women's bodies; the assumption that women's bodies are not something that women themselves have control over. Again, we see this being written into legal structures. In May 2019, 25 US white male politicians made abortion illegal for women in Alabama.[1] These men had made a decision about their control over women's bodies. The fight for women's own reproductive rights has a long history, particularly in so called second wave feminism (repoliticizing debates about abortion, contraception, mothering and feminist ethics of the family).[2] But the underlying assumption that women's bodies are amenable to legal control, or indeed, available to men at any point of their choosing, is something that functions to 'discipline' women and their behaviours.

MeToo/#MeToo invites us to think about the underlying ways in which women are disciplined and controlled through expectations and assumptions about what women are for. The disciplining of women, I will suggest, is one of the mechanisms through which sexism is embedded culturally and patriarchies actively evolve and change over time. Michel Foucault's work is central in thinking about why and how disciplining occurs. While his work implied a gender-neutral space of political control, this chapter seeks to restore gender to the political analysis and argue that this disciplining has a particular gendered form.

Discipline and punish

In *Discipline and Punish*, Michel Foucault explored the way in which discipline was a central feature of regulation; he showed how disciplining of the individual subject was a necessary feature of political systems as a means for maintaining the dominant social order.[3] In his work, Foucault demonstrates how, through the use of fear and terror, those with state power were able to exercise their capacity for punishment as a means to maintain control over the populace. Keep the masses afraid and they will behave. He shows how this first happened through the overt use of public physical violence. (In our current context we see this not only in states inflicting war on other states, but on individual subjects too, for example through the use of the death penalty in some states.) Crucially, however, it was not just the fear of overt physical violence that regulated citizens. Foucault showed how holders of power understood this, and needed other means alongside the threat of overt physical violence to control populations. And so, he argued, surveillance became the mechanism by which states were able to coerce citizens into behaving according to the wishes of the dominant order. To illustrate this, Foucault drew on the idea of a panopticon prison. This was a circular prison with a tower in the centre where at all times prisoners could be watched. However, although the architecture meant that the prisoners could be watched at any time, they themselves did not know when they were being watched. And this became the means by which control was enacted. If prisoners did not know when they were being watched, they would self-regulate and behave as though they were being watched. Prisoners were disciplined into the state's desired form of behaviour, for fear of punishment. Internalizing the idea of surveillance would result in prisoners becoming compliant with the dominant norms and views of behaviour in society. This self-regulation was an effective form of governance, reducing the need for state officials. A regime of governmentality was thus cost effective and self-policing, Foucault argued. This technology of surveillance as a form of control has been insidious in states' maintenance of power over citizens.[4] However, it also takes a particularly gendered form when we start to think about the tools through which the patriarchy is able to discipline and punish women who do not conform to expectations of femininity. Disciplining has taken place in our cultural context through a focus not just on the body, but in particular on women's bodies as a means to reinforce expectations of what women are and what they should be. The woman's body has been a central feature to the understanding of what 'femininity' looks like and by extension a feature of the 'essence' of what it means to be a woman.

Disciplining bodies

Women's bodies are the site where women are disciplined and punished for transgression, regulated and self-regulated. As King notes, 'femininity, is a discipline that produces bodies and identities and operates as an effective form of social control'.[5] The construction of the idea of femininity becomes a crucial mechanism through which women's bodies are positioned as central. It is the *idea* of femininity, rather than the reality, which takes hold and shapes the ways in which women are disciplined. For example a Google image search of the term 'woman's body' generates a set of results that conform to our mediated stereotypes of what women 'should' look like according to our media: white, thin, and with an hourglass figure. All of the images show white women, in underwear/bikinis. The fourth picture along is marked up for cosmetic surgery. All of this serves to remind us that thin and white is the objective, this is what women can do to their bodies, we are told, and by extension, what they should look like; this is the 'normal' body shape for women.

Except we know that it isn't. Only 10 per cent of women have an hourglass body shape, with the majority 63 per cent having a 'rectangle' shape.[6] This mechanism of a focus on women's appearance and body shape perpetuated in and through our media culture has had severe consequences, with threats to life from eating disorders such as anorexia and bulimia to plastic surgery as women are conditioned to find the perfect body and the perfect 'look'.[7] This disciplining of women through a focus on their bodies and appearance is nothing new. In 1990 Naomi Wolf observed the evolution of other mechanisms of controlling women as they advanced legally and materially, and that the greater the gains women made 'the more strictly and heavily and cruelly images of female beauty have come to weigh upon us'.[8]

What Wolf shows us is that the focus on beauty is about controlling and disciplining women's '*behaviour* not appearance'.[9] Women are taught obedience through unattainable standards of beauty. Their worth and objective 'merit' and value in society is determined through their appearance, and focusing attention on unattainable standards of beauty by which women can then be judged as 'failing to meet' means that we regulate women's behaviour as they are encouraged to feel ashamed for not achieving these standards. And of course, if women cannot achieve these standards for themselves, then by implication, how can they possibly achieve in other areas (for example, work, politics, and creating knowledge)? So, the myth of objective merit as a means to assess women's ability is inherently bound up with the ways in which we are encouraged to judge women through ideal bodily standards.

Naomi Wolf's words are as applicable today as at the time of her writing. The regulation of women through their bodies, and the demands for obedience are in evidence not just in existing or traditional media forms, but embedded in the emergent and new technologies of our contemporary society. New social media encourages not just unachievable images of womanhood, but also requires its users to perfect the 'look', take time to comment, upload images, comment on others' images, and follow beauty influencers.[10] Users who fail to meet these ideals are then 'shamed'.[11] But the time, energy and effort required to meet these standards means that not only are women suffering from physical problems such as sleep deprivation and severe impacts upon their physical and mental health; these consequences are far more likely to happen to girls.[12] Moreover, this takes young women away from the very things that would give them a greater sense of their own identity. Social media exacerbates the obsession with image which then becomes a behaviour, a way of life, an end in itself. The search for approval and modification as a function of female appearance is that which self-validation becomes reliant upon. The emphasis on beauty ideals becomes about disciplining women to seek approval.

While women's voices can be silenced and marginalized through a range of mediated, cultural and technological mechanisms (as in the previous chapter) at the same time, the contradiction is that while women's voices are rendered invisible, women's bodies are the sites where women are seen to be validated. Visibility of women is not about what they have to say, or what they think, but what they look like. Where approval and validation is not forthcoming, where women are deemed to have failed to meet the mediated standards of bodily beauty, women are shamed. This in turn, of course, then has an effect on self-esteem. As Sarah Banet-Weiser argues, 'the way that self-esteem becomes legible as a response to shame is by becoming part of the discourse of shame; shame is positioned as a threat or danger to one's self-esteem, therefore it functions as a disciplinary mechanism in perpetuity, there is no point where it might end'.[13] The internalization of self-surveillance and regulation of women's bodies not only functions to control women but also reinforces and reproduces patriarchies through an economic agenda. There has developed a whole industry around developing self-esteem – the 'economy of visibility' in popular feminism relies on women making themselves visible, so that they can identify what is wrong with them and purchase products to resolve these 'problems';[14] problems that are manufactured in and through media culture so that companies can provide the solutions, from the self-help books to the more insidious promotion of cosmetic surgery. Here the focus is on the neoliberal individual women's body, it is for the individual to fix the problem that the system creates and then exposes, rather than for individuals to collectively act (politically) to fix the problem of the system itself.

The solution to the 'problem' of women's bodies and the need for them to fit the idealized standard provided by our mediated cultural industries can be found in cosmetic surgery, we are told by the narratives around us. Women learn, for example, through advertising and media imagery that their most important attribute is their appearance; as noted previously, their beauty and femininity is what 'matters' and this is subject to a narrow interpretation where to be beautiful is to be young, white (or light skinned) and thin. Moreover, women's bodies are turned into commodities, where purchasing products encourages women to imagine that they may achieve unattainable perfection.[15] As Kilbourne argues, women see their face as a mask, their body as separate, but these things are presented as more important than their real selves. We see this not only happening, but happening with huge consequences for women. Research suggests that young girls (aged 13–15) spend a disproportionate amount of time online that is related to internalization of body ideals about thinness and concerns around body image.[16] High use of social media over time has been linked to users' concerns around body image[17] with over 70 per cent of girls in developed nations reporting the desire to be thinner.[18] This clearly has damaging effects on girls' sense of self-worth, and there is a wide-ranging literature that has linked social media usage with body image 'shame' and mental health issues.[19] And yet.

The increasing promotion, popularity and availability of the cosmetics surgery industry means that by the end of 2022 the predictions are that its global worth will be around £8.5 billion.[20] Plastic surgery is clearly big business and while increasing numbers of men are having surgery, the question is raised, why so many women? Market Research Future makes a clear link between the media and cultural industries and the growth in the demand for plastic surgery.[21] Studies also suggest clear links between a woman's dissatisfaction with an area of her body, and her desire to undertake cosmetic surgery to remedy this.[22] It is too simplistic to suggest that this is simply correlated with the increase in social media usage. However, if we situate this in a mediated cultural context where women are surrounded by imagery denoting idealized femininity, where women are judged by their bodies and appearance, we can start to make some sense of this. And these cultural expectations and assumptions are costing women their lives. A study conducted in the US found that 1 in 3,000 women die from an increasingly popular procedure known as a 'Brazilian butt lift'.[23] Moreover, these procedures are reinforcing notions of culturally sexist imperialism; women in Asia and Africa are also having surgery promoted to them as a way in which they can achieve the 'ideal' of white Western femininity.[24] In this sense, we also see how racial features are medicalized in order to make them amenable to cosmetic surgery,[25] while at the same time reinforcing white masculine norms and values of womanhood.

So on the one hand women are surrounded with idealized images of what it means to be a woman; and that revolves entirely around physical appearance of whiteness, unattainable body shapes and youth. On the other, industry benefits from providing the 'solution' to the dissatisfaction created through advertising which promotes the same narratives as our cultural industries. Of course women are going to be dissatisfied and unhappy if they are continually told that the only thing that matters about them is how they look, and then, because they do not look like the super models, influencers and TV stars who embody this look, and if industries are providing a solution for a problem they created, it becomes a self-fulfilling prophecy. Naomi Wolf offers the analogy that 'an economy that depends on slavery needs to promote images of slaves that "justify" the institution of slavery'.[26] And so our economy promotes ideals and standards of beauty as the requirement for what it is to be a woman. That is, if a woman is regulated and measured by her appearance she will behave accordingly, and remain vulnerable to approval; reliant on people other than herself for a sense of self-worth.

But it is not only in the beauty industry that women are subjected to disciplining of their bodies. In August 2018, Boris Johnson (following his resignation as UK Foreign Secretary in July of that year) provoked anger using his column in *The Telegraph* to vilify and target Muslim women. His offensive comments including statements such as: 'It is absolutely ridiculous that people should choose to go around looking like letter boxes' and compared women wearing the burqa to bank robbers.[27] While media outrage ensued, and Johnson refused to apologize, what was noticeable here was the sense of entitlement Johnson appeared to have; his self-certainty of eligibility to comment upon women and their bodies. And this largely takes the form of one of two tropes. On the one hand, women who wear the veil are viewed, in Western terms, as oppressed. The 'white saviour' narrative comes into play, and has been used politically as justification to intervene in foreign policy and wars by UK governments.[28] Ignoring colonial histories, 'saving women' becomes a means by which women are mechanisms through which to demonize 'other' Muslim men. These women, the narrative goes, need to be rescued from the barbarism of the men in their countries and cultures, conveniently ignoring the ways in which white men in our own countries and cultures reinforce misogyny. Analysis of media discourses has raised concern about the levels of Islamophobia we witness in our newspaper headlines (and elsewhere).[29] However, the second trope is that these women should not be seen or heard at all and when they do appear it is only in connection with violence inflicted upon them. As Baroness Saeeyda Warsi notes:

> more often than not, Muslim women are only heard in public life, or in the media, when we fit an existing narrative or reinforce a lazy stereotype. If the story's about polygamy, FGM, forced marriages or – most often – the burqa – you'll hear Muslim women on the radio. It sometimes seems that we are only seen as the sum total of our bad experiences.[30]

As a recent book *It's Not About the Burqa* reminds us, through a wonderful collection of Muslim women's voices, as with other women, Muslim women experience multiple sites of politics being played out in and through their bodies.[31]

Discipline in public spaces

Figure 6.1 shows a picture of a building that I work in.

Figure 6.1: Image of workplace

The first thing women are taught by this building is how to dress. Because when female staff have to do open days, or teach, or female students come to learn, they cannot wear a skirt. And they cannot wear skirts as someone can take a photo from under the stairs (from that handily positioned seat/photo op spot) and post it on Facebook, to humiliate, shame, and expose. Upskirting has recently been criminalized in the UK, thanks to the hard work of campaigner Gina Martin.[32] However, there are no signs telling men not to take upskirt photos. What there is, is the expectation of the self-regulation of women, in public spaces.

We regularly see women disciplined and self-disciplined in public spaces. Women have to learn to walk with keys in their hands in case they are attacked. Women are disciplined in public spaces to feel 'the right amount of panic'.[33] But this is the wrong message! Shouldn't we be telling men not to behave like this in the first place? Many women can tell stories of being mansplained to, having their personal space invaded, men deciding that despite the wearing of headphones women want to talk to them, being followed, being touched without having been asked.[34] These everyday micro aggressions form the basis not simply of making women feel uncomfortable and wary of their place in the world but of disciplining women into accepting this as their role. And through this isolation women are disciplined into silence and submission.

Fiona Vera-Gray offers a systematic analysis of the ways in which street harassment teaches women to exhibit 'the right amount of panic'.[35] That is, women learn their place, the expectations placed upon them, and self-regulate, self-discipline to keep themselves safe. They regulate their behaviour according to their expectations of being harassed or abused. Vera-Gray's work shows that the perception of street harassment is far greater than the actuality of the experience. While on the one hand this might provide some comfort that street harassment is maybe less prevalent than we might think, at the same time, the key is that women perceive the threat of street harassment to be real. This perception does the work required of the patriarchy. So irrespective of its actuality, women are conditioned to do the necessary work required to keep themselves safe. And it is an interesting positioning, rather than men internalizing an expectation that they should not street harass or indeed present the perception of a threat to women.

Discipline as symbolic violence

This systemic governance of women, internalized as self-regulation of bodies in private and public spaces, takes the form, we could argue, of a symbolic violence. For Bourdieu, symbolic systems are a mechanism, if not *the* mechanism for constructing what we understand as 'reality'.[36] Bourdieu expands on the notion of symbolic systems to incorporate the idea of symbolic violence. He suggests that symbolic systems are not neutral. They rely on power relationships, domination and subordination. He argues that systems of unequal power relations and exploitation are reproduced through daily practice. Through the ways in which we interact and engage with 'reality'. It is through both our cultural actions and our cultural experiences that these relations of power are normalized.[37] For Bourdieu, this constitutes a form of violence. The notion of symbolic violence also helps us understand the ways in which the oppressed become complicit in their own oppression ... and certain assumptions and behaviours become normalized, such as the ideal body type that women are seeking to achieve. If we want to understand why women focus so much attention on their appearance, we might want to think about the systemic ways in which they are encouraged to do so, and then do so (apparently) willingly. Why do women do the work of displaying the 'right amount of panic' to stay safe? What we might take from Bourdieu, is that women are unable to recognize (or escape) their own complicity in a system which reinforces women's oppression.

Kate Millet wrote of the ways in which these power relations are ideologically reinforced through popular culture and literature. In particular she notes the ways in which power is sustained through consent or through violence; the ideological reproduction of consent is achieved through socialization into patriarchal politics.[38] Taking this one step further we might see how this consent itself becomes a form of violence. Once ideology functions to manufacture consent, and power structures become invisible, then we are in the realm of symbolic violence. For Bourdieu, symbolic violence is not only about the enacting of violence through structures, but the ways in which we give consent to that violence being enacted; that we become complicit in our own oppression. This is illustrated through examples of what is taken for granted as knowledge: that women deserve to be paid less for example, or that women are better at cooking or cleaning; that there are certain jobs that women are not good enough to do. These taken-for-granted forms of knowledge occur because as Bourdieu argues the 'mind is constructed according to the cognitive structures that are issued out of the very structures of the world'.[39] That is, the beliefs we hold about the 'natural order' of things are so ingrained they become ideological, we become complicit, because the structures around us socialize us into taking these assumptions for granted.

Discipline and violence: violence as a continuum

Symbolic violence within structures, which becomes manifested in notions of 'common sense' matters if we are to consider the role that is also being played in legitimating physical violence. If we are to think of the disciplining and silencing of women justified through meritocratic discourses as forms of gendered violence, then it might be useful to think about how we define said violence. Clearly when we use the term violence we have different perceptions of what that might mean. Liz Kelly offers a continuum definition of sexual violence which draws attention to the 'wider range of forms of abuse and assault which women experience' between the 'everyday' and the 'extremes'.[40] For Kelly, this continuum approach is effective in a twofold way: first in discussing the range of ways in which men use a variety of forms of abuse, coercion and force to control women; but second, giving women the vocabulary and language to name and describe their experiences.[41] What this continuum definition also highlights is that there is not necessarily a hierarchy of severity of violence, but we need to take into account the differential impacts and effects that different types of violence have on different women.[42] A micro aggression may be something that is shrugged off, but its cumulative effect is to normalize and legitimate greater scales and magnitudes of violence: as has been so amply illustrated through MeToo/#MeToo.

Building on this continuum definition however, it is argued here that the expression of violence is not simply something which is done by men to women. Rather this is also something that is embedded within our structures. It is argued that symbolic and epistemic violence underlie and underpin the agency that is possible and likely within our social, cultural and media structures. This symbolic violence takes the form of disciplining women through their bodies and through the physical world that is built around us and its reinforcement and communication. The epistemic silencing of women and their knowledge is also integrated into the structure. That we give 'consent' or become complicit in these violent structures, in turn lays the groundwork for the normalization of physical and other forms of violence.

A continuum definition of violence also allows us to make explicit how disciplining and silencing form part of the coercion/consent necessary for the maintenance and legitimation of more physical forms of violence. That is, discipline and consent do the work of normalizing epistemic and symbolic violence, which puts violence at the heart of structures to the extent that we are not aware of these systems structured around violence. This then normalizes and lessens the degree to which we see these actions as violent, and also normalizes the ways in which material (physical) violence becomes part of our psyche and cultural norms and practices (as discussed in the following chapter).

Conclusion

Disciplining functions as a mechanism of gendered control. Once we internalize the ways in which patriarchal structures expect us to behave, we do the work of the patriarchy in internalizing sexism and misogyny; we self-discipline, self-police, self-regulate, we self-govern. One of the ways in which women are taught to do the work of the patriarchy is through the overt regulation of their bodies. Where women's voices and interests are silenced and marginalized, their bodies are sites of heightened visibility. But the disciplining of women's bodies and the silencing of women's voices are part of a cumulative pattern of the regulation of women. Women who transgress these norms are punished, 'shamed' and made invisible. The ageing of women's bodies, for example, has long been something which our contemporary media cannot deal with. In 25 films nominated for best picture in 2017, less than 2.6 per cent of roles were held by women over 60.[43] And where they were depicted, they were in far less powerful jobs than their male counterparts. *Time* magazine notes how men reach their 'peak roles at the age of 46, women at 30'.[44] At 37 Maggie Gyllenhaal was told she was 'too old' to appear opposite a 55 year old James Bond, and Helen Mirren commented, 'as James Bond got more and more geriatric, his girlfriends got younger and younger'.[45]

MeToo/#MeToo drew attention not just to physical expressions of assault, abuse and harassment, but the underlying assumptions of entitlement of some men to have the right to power, control over women's bodies and voices. Where our media constructions are focused on masculine ideals of what women are for, and what women can be, women also can repoliticize this issue by reclaiming the right to their bodies (as they did in and through the MeToo/#MeToo movement). The disciplining of women through the focus on their bodies, I have suggested here, functions as a form of symbolic violence. Violence runs through and underpins our patriarchal structures, and takes a range of differing forms. It is the cumulative effect of the disciplining of women's bodies (symbolically) and the silencing of women's voices (epistemically) that form the basis by which the legitimation of physical violence towards women takes place.

7

Violence

History is grounded in rape and male sexual violence against women. bell hooks details the systematic and horrific rapes of Black women by white slave owners.[1] Danielle McGuire provides a compelling account of the shocking levels of rape and male sexual violence inflicted by white men on Black women as a central driver within the civil rights movement (and yet so notably written out of these histories).[2] We see this history of violence contained in the myths that we tell about our society, and some recent contemporary fiction has rewritten these myths from the female perspective.[3] That female perspective highlights how women's experiences were characterized by rape and male sexual violence upon women's bodies. What is notable is the ways in which assumptions about rape and male sexual violence against women have not only shaped legislation (written by and for predominantly white men) but how these understandings about rape are enshrined within culture.

Susan Brownmiller wrote: 'from prehistoric times to the present … rape has played a critical function. It is nothing more or less than a conscious process of intimidation by which *all* men keep *all* women in a state of fear'.[4] Rape is a process not only of physical control, but a political means of enforcing a system of control over women through fear of physical control. The idea that rape is a legitimate mechanism of controlling women, it would seem, is part of our cultural discourse. Mediated 'rape culture' has served to normalize and legitimate male sexual violence towards a diversity of women.[5] Building on the notions of symbolic violence (the disciplining and regulation of women's bodies) and epistemic violence (the silencing and marginalization of women's voices) I suggest that these forms of violence play a role in the continuation of the cultural normalization of male sexual violence towards and against women.

#MeToo has brought into sharp focus the consequences of this normalization. Women are reclaiming their agency as they refuse to be silenced about rape and sexual violence. Roxanne Gay and Sohaila Abdulali provide us with personalized accounts and reflections of the damage, the huge consequences and impact that rape has had on their lives.[6] They reflect on the nuance and reactions of themselves and others when they talk about rape and the mix of shame and disbelief that they have felt. But then talk of honour and compassion toward yourself and the compassion of others. Abdulali also reminds us of the importance of speaking up, when you are ready. But this process of speaking up and speaking out, bearing testimony, as the African-American women in the precursor to the civil rights movement did, is something which both Gay and Abdulali remind us is immensely powerful.

While women are claiming and regaining control, at the same time, imagery of sexual violence towards women has become ever more freely and frequently available. Kat Banyard details the ways in which this has been normalized through a 'pornification' of internet culture.[7] At least 200 million women alive today have been subjected to genital mutilation. Women and girls account for 71 per cent of human trafficking worldwide, with nearly three out of every four being trafficked for sexual exploitation.[8] We might not only ask how it is possible for this to happen, but why it is that these levels of violence do not generate wider public discussion and outrage? How does male sexual violence towards and against women become so normalized? This chapter discusses these questions in relation not only to media culture but also the role of the state in legitimating discourses of masculinized violence towards women.

Prevalence and normalization of male sexual violence

There was no indication as to why the photo shown in Figure 7.1 was being used to identify toilet facilities.

Figure 7.1: Image of signage on café toilet door

However, this sign does invite us to see as normal the idea that men have the right to invade women's private and personal space. This sign also tells us that this invasion of women's space is something that is funny. This sign also claims that despite this, it is okay, because they are actually 'safe' to use the toilets. That a further sign is displayed that feels the need to spell out safety, demonstrates an awareness perhaps of just how violent this kind of imagery is and the potential consequences of such imagery. According to UN data, just over one in ten girls worldwide have experienced forced intercourse and/or sexual acts.[9] If we situate this sign in the wider context of violence against women as a 'normal' and everyday phenomenon then maybe it is not quite so funny.

According to a 2018 Amnesty International report, approximately nine million women have been raped since the age of 15.[10] Across the EU only eight countries (and three of those are in the UK) recognize that sex without consent is rape.[11] In the UK, the Crime Survey for England and Wales estimated that 20 per cent of women and 4 per cent of men have experienced some type of sexual assault since the age of 16, equivalent to an estimated 3.4 million female victims and 631,000 male victims. Of these victims, 83 per cent did not report their experience to the police.[12] In 2018, despite the doubling of the number of reported rapes since 2013–14, the number charged with rape fell by 23.1 per cent compared to 2017. While the prosecution of rape is falling, rape crisis centres are reporting an increase of 17 per cent in the numbers accessing their services during the same time period.[13]

In the UK women can be jailed for false allegations of male rape.[14] The occurrences of false allegations are rare. A Ministry of Justice report estimated that in the UK, only 3 per cent of rape reports were perceived to be unfounded.[15] In the US, a study in 2010 demonstrated that in the previous 20 years only between 2–10 per cent of reported rapes were determined to be 'false'.[16] In the US, 'false' reporting is treated as a minor misdemeanour by police rather than grounds for prosecution.[17] However, in the UK women can be prosecuted for perverting the course of justice, which carries a maximum life sentence term.[18] In 2011–12 a report to the Director of Public Prosecutions concerned with the issue of false allegations of rape and domestic violence observed that:

> in the period of the review, there were 5,651 prosecutions for rape and 111,891 for domestic violence. During the same period there were 35 prosecutions for making false allegations of rape, 6 for making false allegation of domestic violence and 3 for making false allegations of both rape and domestic violence.[19] The percentage of false rape allegations prosecuted in one year was 0.62 per cent.

And yet, media coverage would have us believe that false rape allegations are a major societal problem. Newspaper headlines give front page status to cases where false accusations of rape have been prosecuted. For example, in 2017 the London *Metro* ran with a headline which read '10 years for woman who cried rape'. And opened with:

> A FANTASIST who falsely accused nine men of rape was jailed for ten years ... Judge Nicholas Loraine-Smith said as he sentenced her. 'You are a very, very convincing liar and you enjoy being seen as a victim ... What is particularly chilling is the manner in which you persisted in making allegations which you knew were untrue, even to the extent of committing and repeating perjury.[20]

The sensationalism of this report, and the way we are invited to judge the female defendant, Jemma Beale, diverge markedly with the ways in which a man being accused of perjury is treated. Let us contrast this construction of a woman as a 'fantasist' with the ways in which media discussed the trial of police officer Brian Encinia. Encinia is the police officer who arrested Sandra Bland in 2015 for a minor traffic violation. She died in a police cell three days later. The *Daily Mail* reported:

> A Texas state trooper has been indicted for perjury in the case of black police detainee Sandra Bland who died in custody last summer. Bland was found dead in a jail cell in Waller County, Texas, three days after she was arrested for a traffic stop in July, 2014. Her family filed a lawsuit, accusing Waller police of subjected [sic] her to unwarranted brutality in custody. Today a grand jury voted to indict Texas State Trooper Brian Encinia, who arrested the 28-year-old, during a traffic stop, for perjury.[21]

Despite both Encinia and Beale being prosecuted for perjury, we are invited to read and to respond to what they have done in very different ways. While Beale is described as a fantasist,

Encinia is described in professional terms. He is not described as liar or chilling. We are invited to ignore the fact that his behaviour resulted in the loss of a young Black woman's life. But we are encouraged as audiences to view him in professional, non-emotive terms. For his charge of perjury, it is possible that he could have faced a maximum of one year in jail, in contrast to the possible life sentence that can be imposed upon women being found guilty of false rape allegations in the UK. Under the headline 'Rape lies end in jail term' the *Oxford Mail* reports how a woman convicted of perjury was 'betraying the sisterhood'.[22] I do not see reports of the judge berating Encinia, or any other man accused of perjury, as betraying the brotherhood or patriarchy.

Rape myths

The notion that women routinely falsify rape allegations is widespread and plays a key role in sustaining rape myths. It was Lord Hale in the 17th century who originally remarked that, 'in a rape case it is the victim, not the defendant, who is on trial'.[23] As Williams has observed, 'for some crimes, robbery for example, the victim's responsibility is rarely questioned, but for rape the victim's responsibility is mostly always questioned'.[24] This questioning of the victim's role and responsibility in their violation feeds into public opinion. While rape myths are more likely to be accepted by men than women,[25] nonetheless they have been linked to low levels of conviction of perpetrators, and the sustained disbelief of women reporting rape as a crime.[26] Rape myths suggest that women actually enjoy being raped; they also function to legitimate and reinforce the notion that there are 'blurred lines' around the idea of consent.[27]

These myths are reinforced through the ways in which our media talk about male sexual violence. Cindy Carter's analysis shows us that there has been a historical increase in media actually talking about sexual violence.[28] However, the tone of this coverage has done nothing to dispel rape myths. Carter shows how coverage has been increasingly sexualized, so as to be 'titillating' for the (assumed male) reader and that stories of sexual violence are interlinked with stories of sexual gossip. In *The Sun* and *News of the World*, reports have been placed near to images of Page 3 girls,[29] and in the *Daily Star*, on front pages next to pictures of women in bikinis.[30] Moreover, Carter notes the disproportionate coverage on murder and rape at the expense of domestic violence (when compared to police statistics). She also found that coverage of male rape of women tended to reinforce the 'stranger' myth. Rape reported where the man was known to the woman was seen as 'too ordinary' to warrant media attention. This type of framing, as Carter argues, encourages readers to accept unsensationalized violence towards women as typical, inevitable features of daily life. While this work was conducted a number of years ago, we find that in some ways, little seems to have changed to improve the position of and for women in this coverage.

Karen Boyle builds on this work by exploring how victims of male sexual violence are depicted in media when they do appear. She demonstrates how the focus on a female victim's perceived attractiveness becomes an essential feature of the story; using victims who are represented as attractive is a mechanism designed to generate greater sympathy from the audience, and therefore be deemed 'newsworthy'. Boyle demonstrates how this framing is in complete opposition to the ways in which male victims are depicted. Where male victims feature they are simply not discussed in ways that emphasize their attractiveness, desirability, or behaviour at the time of the assault.[31] Not only do these media narratives reinforce simplistic assumptions about women's appearance and behaviour, about what women should be (virgins) and should not do (for instance, drink), they make distinctions between deserving and undeserving rape victims. Those women who do not conform to mediated ideals of womanhood, it would seem fall into the undeserving category. Moreover, this woman is always assumed to be white, and is unlikely to be portrayed at all if she is Black.[32]

Intersectional analysis enables us to see how the 'ideal' rape victim is presented. In India, coverage is focused on the middle class victim, marginalizing the poor, lower caste victims. Moreover, this coverage, Shakuntala Rao argues, reinforces a politics and ethics of shame, where women's presence in public spaces is already viewed with hostility.[33] In 2015, Meena Seshu of SANGRAM reported findings of sexual violence against sex workers in Asia. What is alarming and noticeable, was not the levels of violence but the silence with which this report was met. In an interview with Sohaila Abdulali she says:

> 'it was launched in Bangkok – nobody wrote about it. It was launched in Myanmar – nobody wrote about it. The UN distributes it – nobody writes about it. The media came to all the events. People for TV, people from newspapers – they interviewed people like the study's interviewers, who were all sex workers themselves. And then nobody wrote about it.'[34]

It might seem that media do not really want to talk about some of the wider issues that underpin male sexual violence; that sex workers somehow are seen as not 'worthy' rape victims for media coverage. It is a scandal that an estimated 16 million women suffer from domestic violence each year, but less than 10 per cent of them go to the police.[35] And we are still not widely having public discussions about why men rape, rather than why this victim deserved or did not deserve to be raped.

Where we do see coverage which speaks of the perpetrators of violence towards women this is framed very differently. Media coverage of news stories can often marginalize the perpetrator (as in the case where we are invited to sympathize with a family man driven to commit a terrible act and women who are invisible in the stories). A Fox News headline published on 30 May 2019 to promote a forthcoming documentary is illustrative: 'Chris Watts' horrific killings of wife, daughters still haunt investigators, new doc reveals'.[36] His wife and daughters are not even named until near the very end of the piece. This removal of their names removes our sympathies for them as actual people, they are framed to us as simply nondescript, invisible, irrelevant to the main point of focus.

The killing of women is often accompanied by an explanation of the man's good character. BBC News ran the headline in May 2019 that 'Farnham puppy farm murderer John Lowe "was a father figure"'.[37] That is, John Lowe who had taken a gun to kill Christine Lee and Lucy Lee, in 2014, we are told through the courts and media coverage of this case, was previously someone who had been thought of as kind. We are invited to see, to understand, and somehow sympathize with men who take women's lives. Yet we do not see this kind of sympathy of coverage with men who take the lives of others in terrorist attacks. It is still men committing violence. The difference is that this violence is happening to invisible women. Our media reportage operates, it seems, with a very simplistic binary in respect of male violence against women. If the focus is on a male perpetrator, then the female victim is rendered invisible. And as Boyle demonstrates, if the focus is on the female victim, then she is required to have attained masculinized ideals of femininity.[38] An overemphasis on false allegations and the questioning of a victim's behaviour might suggest that we are more likely to believe that a woman is 'making it up'. And if the focus is on the crime of sexual violence, then we are invited to read this in a wider cultural discourse of rape myths, normalized in and through our popular culture.

Rape culture

Male rape of women is a common plotline used to drive narratives forward in film and TV.[39] Viewing this type of television programming has been demonstrated to increase the acceptance of rape myths and the prevalence of false rape allegations among audiences.[40] At the same time, this viewing did not lead to an overestimation of the amount of rape that took place in society.[41] So while false allegations of rape were assumed to be common, male rape of women was not assumed to be a widespread problem. In her detailed study of primetime programming depictions of rape, Lisa Cuklanz argues that the primary function of the showing of rape on TV during the 1970s and 1980s was to contain feminist arguments about rape which were taking place at the time (through the works of Dworkin and MacKinnon for example) and reassert dominant forms of masculinity.[42] Depictions of rape in film have been argued to reinforce unidimensional rape myths that rape is largely something done by sadistic strangers, rather than by someone who is known to the victim.[43]

In their work on the use of metaphors to discuss how people 'make sense' of rape, psychologists Anderson and Doherty conducted studies where they explored how people talked about rape.[44] Their findings were startling. They found that the language of science was part of the discourse around the rape of women. Rape of women was something that was seen as 'predictable' and was high in 'probability'. Male rape of men, however, was discursively discussed as deviant, 'bizarre' and 'weird'. Why do we consider female rape as likely, and to an extent, to be expected? Rather than weird, bizarre or abhorrent? In relation to the ways in which rape myths are normalized, scholars and feminist activists have long discussed the problem of 'rape culture'.[45] Rape culture is that which is underpinned by

> a complex of beliefs that encourage male sexual aggression and [support] violence against women [and girls], a society where violence is seen as sexy and sexuality as violent, and a continuum of threatened violence that ranges from sexual remarks to sexual touching to rape itself. A rape culture condones physical and emotional terrorism against women [and girls] and presents it as the norm.[46]

This definition is useful in reflecting the complexity and nuance of the insidious ways in which male sexual violence towards women is normalized in our cultural context. The ways in which media present this to us fundamentally play a key role in reinforcing and normalizing this set of expectations and assumptions.

In 2013 two young men took photographs and videos of their rape and sexual abuse of a young woman in Steubenville, US. The images went viral and a court case ensued. What was depressing and perhaps all too familiar was the way in which media responses were framed. Here, as Laurie Penny observes, was rape being 'condoned, encouraged [and] celebrated'.[47] The defence and media discourse drew outrage for their focus on the damage that would be done to the perpetrators who were positioned as 'two young men that had such promising futures, star football players, very good students'.[48] We are invited to feel sympathy, in this kind of positioning for men who commit these violent acts, in a way that just does not happen in respect of other crimes.

In 2006, 14-year-old Abeer Qassim Hamza al-Janabi was raped and murdered by US soldiers, near the village Yusufiyah, in Baghdad province. Her father, mother and five year old sister were also killed. Abeer's body was set on fire after she was killed. Western media coverage focused on the stories of the defendants, and the stresses of being in the armed forces.[49] Like the Steubenville case, we are encouraged to take a sympathetic reading of these men's behaviour and violence towards women as a release from stress. In an article published by CNN.com (see excerpt to follow) we see the headline and opening paragraph in bold, directing our attention and our sympathies to men under huge amounts of stress. We are invited to read this as a defence justification of men's actions. The primary focus in the story in the first paragraph seeks to elicit sympathy. It is the second paragraph, which positions this of lesser importance, that sanitizes the brutal rapes and murder of a young girl and her family.

Soldier: 'Death walk' drives troops 'nuts'

BAGHDAD, IRAQ (CNN) – Defense attorneys in a military rare-murder hearing on Tuesday emphasized the stress defendants faced, with one private testifying that soldiers consumed whiskey and painkillers to try to cope with duty in Iraq.

Four soldiers are charged in connection with the rape of an Iraqi and the killing of her and her family.[50]

The young woman is not named, and is invisibilized through the use of her nationality, rather than her age and gender. And we might ask, can we imagine any other forms of crime being justified, defended and legitimated by the stress that the aggressor was suffering?

In 2018 the head of the UK police force made a statement suggesting that police forces should focus their resources on burglary and violent crime, rather than logging hate crimes against women.[51] This was justified in the interests of 'public safety'. And yet over 50 per cent of the population are women. Do these 50 per cent not constitute the public, and their concerns for public safety? Much violent crime is perpetrated by men. Why are we not labelling crime in gendered terms? If we start to discuss it in these terms, we can start to see where the problems lie. Work around the demonization of people of colour has pointed to the ways in which media discourses would label crime perpetrators by their race, when their race was not white.[52] So a 'murderer' was assumed to be a white male, and 'othered' when the perpetrator was a person of colour: a Black murderer. So people of colour have been othered by the inclusion of their race in the reportage. We now witness this taking place in the discourse around terrorism. When the perpetrators are assumed to have committed a terrorist act, they are referred to as Muslim; when the perpetrator is white, this is referred to predominantly in mental health terms or as a 'lone wolf' act.[53] Yet what all of these discussions miss is that it is largely *men* who are carrying out these acts. Reporting these acts in gendered terms, such as Man Plants Bomb, or Man Murders Woman, enables a much clearer insight in to how this violence occurs. There is a gendered dimension to the levels of violence that we see and experience. And yet, this gendered dimension is obscured and normalized through the language that we use and the ways in which we talk about male violence in our media and in our political structures. Male violence against women is legitimated in our media cultures and it is sanctioned politically through the state use of sexual violence as a weapon of warfare, which both underpins and interacts with our normalization of rape, and rape culture.

Rape and warfare

War memorials and war crimes point us to numbers of dead men. We have memorial services and shrines to fallen soldiers who have fought for our freedoms. At the same time, we have also had women who, unrecognized, have suffered in the name of this fight for 'our freedom' but they remain broadly invisible. Women's roles and experiences have often been written out of international politics and analysis.[54] In narratives around war, where women do appear the most prominent positioning is as that of a victim. The function of this positioning is to reify the duty of the male soldier to protect the woman, from torture or death.[55] It is this heavily masculinized narrative of strength and protection, rather than sexual violence, that underpins our popular narratives about the conduct of war. Where abuse of women is discussed this is often framed as a means to support political strategies and rhetoric, rather than as analysis or outrage at the systematic abject violence and abuse of women.[56]

One way we might repoliticize this issue is to ask, who creates war, and in whose interests? These questions direct us to look at political leaders (mainly white men) and the interests of the arms industry, generating billions of dollars of profit. It might be simple to suggest that a world run by women as heads of states would not result in war. Indeed, to suggest that if women were all of the world leaders we would not necessarily see warfare is to assume a biological pacifism. The aim here is not to suggest war flows from biological function. However, what is perhaps of interest here is how we as societies value the contributions of those in war. Who counts as making 'legitimate' contributions to warfare? The soldiers who die because they fought the enemy? Or the women who are raped, brutalized and imprisoned to serve the purpose of the army.[57] Armed conflict, the preserve of the state, operates to marginalize and silence the roles of women and the impact of war on them through the reification of the masculine contribution; while simultaneously silencing the experiences of women who lost their lives, and had their lives destroyed because of this sexualized violence against them. For example, between 1932 and 1945, imperial Japan abducted and forced tens of thousands of women, from Korea and China, into prostitution to service the military.[58] They sanitized this by calling them 'comfort' women. Records of this abuse are scarce although it is estimated that more than 90 per cent of these women did not survive the war.[59]

Not only does the state play a role in normalizing masculinized violence but this is perpetuated through the glamorization of war in our media culture. Women's experiences in war are highly misrepresented in media and subject to 'news blackout'.[60] As Nordstrom observes there have been hundreds of thousands of texts dissecting and analyzing war, yet only a tiny percentage focus on rape.[61] Rape as a weapon of warfare is written out of legal constitutions, for example on genocide, despite sharing similarities in definition.[62] The writing out of rape is further reinforced through our cultural climate. The 'noble war fantasy' is reinforced through video gaming, where digital war games reinforce political narratives of perpetual war.[63] A perpetual war of, and underpinned by, masculine violence. It has been demonstrated that video gaming with high levels of sexual violence towards women has functioned to increase acceptance of 'rape myths'.[64] We are training our young people to accept sexual violence as the norm. Excluding the violence that men do to women in warfare from our narratives serves to silence these experiences, and by extension, if we cannot see them they do not exist. If they do not exist they cannot be happening. And if we are not talking about them happening, they become normalized and routinized. They are acceptable means of dealing with stress, apparently. The language of war is not confined to media coverage of state violence. In current political discourse, parties are 'weaponizing the NHS' declaring 'war on poverty' or 'war on benefits scroungers' depending on their ideological positioning (as noted in Chapter 4). But in using the masculinized language of violence and warfare, they reinforce the legitimacy of violence, the legitimacy of war premised on female oppression, exploitation and subjugation. Sanitizing sexual violence by failing to discuss it does not make it okay.

Conclusion

Media culture plays a fundamental role in normalizing male sexual violence towards women. The term male sexual violence is used to restore the agency of the perpetrator to the action, and the term women is used to render the person to whom the action is inflicted visible. Violence towards and against women is an enormous societal problem, and yet is sanctioned by states, and normalized in the legitimate force used by states in times of war. Masculinity is emphasized in war games and films; we simply do not really talk about (or indeed often prosecute) those who engage in this act. There is not one simple source of 'rape culture' but media, popular culture and states interact in a space where rape myths endure.

This has resulted in a cultural context where sexual violence towards women has been normalized, legitimated and sanctioned. In contrast, sexual violence towards men is met with horror, seen as an aberration. This gendered legitimation of violence is reinforced symbolically in its representation. Not only are we taught that women can be violated, often with impunity, but this is a mechanism of maintaining and disciplining an established social and political order. Politically, to restore gender to our analysis means to restore the voices and experiences of women. In making women and their experiences visible we can see the underlying politically gendered power structures, which are upheld through narratives of violence. What MeToo/#MeToo has enabled us to see, like the African-American women in the civil rights movement, is how powerful it can be when women speak up and out. If we think about what those women achieved in the power of their testimonies to underpin the change that was effected through the civil rights movement, let us just think about what we can learn from that and how we can harness the power of women and their testimonies and repoliticize sexism.

Conclusion: The Politics of Feminist Rage

This book started with a question: what has really changed since MeToo/#MeToo? The aim was to expose the myriad ways in which sexism is woven into and through our mediated culture. These structures have real world consequences and effects which serve to silence, marginalize and discipline us to accept a system of violence towards women. Except. We don't have to accept this, and these 'fuck you' moments have been very much part of the discourse around #MeToo.[1] The question then becomes how do we channel this sentiment, and harness rage to empower us, rather than let it become our own undoing? In this final chapter I focus on three elements necessary for this change in our conversation and our cultural structures: rage, reversing and repoliticizing.

Rage

Germaine Greer said, 'women have very little idea of how much men hate them'.[2] This hatred has been legitimated through the sexist structures that male entitlement has built around us as a society. Audre Lorde writes, 'we are Black women born into a society of entrenched loathing and contempt for whatever is Black and female'.[3] If we take hatred of women, in all of their diverse forms, as a starting point, we can see how misogyny seeps through structures which serve to reinforce a particular type of masculine entitlement.

This male entitlement has been evident in the response to MeToo/#MeToo.[4] When male perpetrators are exposed there are expressions of anger at the penalties imposed upon them. We are encouraged to feel sympathy for these men at the 'injustice' that has been visited upon them; after all, they were just behaving 'as lads do'. Kate Manne terms this expectation of sympathy and support for men who have engaged in sexual harassment and violence, 'himpathy'.[5] Brett Kavanaugh's rage and explosive anger at the testimony of Dr Christine Blasey Ford elicited 'himpathy' from Donald Trump and some members of the Republican party.[6] Feminist theorizing and activism shows us just how important anger can be in challenging this entitlement. Anger and rage have re-entered academic and public debates and the feminist lexicon. Recent books and articles confront assumptions about who is entitled to legitimately be angry.[7] Women are in a system not designed for them; we should all be angry. We can be angry, creative and change the conversation. Because as MeToo/#MeToo reminds us, we really do need to change this conversation.

Helen Wood argues for an irreverent rage that we need to externalize; this she encapsulates through her discussion of the increasing use of the term 'fuck you' as an important basis of contemporary feminist response to the climates women find themselves in.[8] The expression 'fuck you' suggests an individual action, one person or group, speaking to another individual. I argue that the term 'fuck this' broadens this anger and becomes a means of repoliticization and of collective action. It rails against a world in which female genital mutilation is still taking place, affecting an estimated 137,000 women in the UK (not including those who are 'hidden');[9] where rape is a weapon of war;[10] and where women are subjected to daily humiliations and sexual violations because of their appearance. The phrase is a call to arms and rejection of the status quo. Using the language of offense ensures that people will take notice, and so women have both directly and indirectly been saying 'fuck you' and 'fuck this' in response to individual men who perpetrate and violate and to a system of privilege that silences, disciplines and marginalizes them.

Reflecting on the #MeToo experience also enables us to observe other emotions that are an inevitable part of the feminist experience and which need to be incorporated into rage. The first is despair. Despair that things may not change, that we will have this moment and then be back to sexism as usual. Despair is deepened by that fact that feminist rage itself can be a further means of silencing women. Women are dismissed as 'shrill' or 'shouty'. Women's anger can be silenced, delegitimized and disallowed. Thus, ironically, anger becomes both a feature of the embedding of sexism and the possibility of its undoing. To ensure it leads to change, what needs to be maintained is the more powerful component: hope. The sense that things could be different, and better, if we harness the creative energies and angers of women. Jilly Boyce Kay and Sarah Banet-Weiser encapsulate this tension wonderfully with their restoration of the term 'respair'. Respair, they argue, 'points to the inextricability of hope and despair that is entailed in any feminist endeavour'.[11] And it is the combination of these two features – hope and a recovery from despair – which is necessary for the undoing of the sexism around us. Respair needs to be a key feature of rage if it is to play a role in the reversal and undoing of sexism.

Reversing

What does it look like to reverse sexism? A good example of the way in which it can be reversed and changed comes from Nottingham in the UK. Here activists and academics have successfully managed to get the local police force to recognize misogyny as a hate crime. In the two-year period following the introduction of the policy of recording misogyny as a hate crime, there were 174 reported misogyny hate crimes.[12] Having undertaken a survey of those who had reported such crimes it was found that examples included 'sexual assault, which had been experienced by 24.7% of survey respondents; indecent exposure (25.9%); groping (46.2%); taking unwanted photographs on mobiles (17.3%); upskirting (6.8%); online abuse (21.7%); being followed home (25.2%); whistling (62.9%); sexually explicit language (54.3%); threatening/aggressive/intimidating behaviour (51.8%); and unwanted sexual advances (48.9%)'.[13] These reporting mechanisms and stories of successful outcomes are a consequence of the political activism coordinated by the Nottingham Women's Centre, the University of Nottingham and Nottingham Trent University. In changing procedures, they are paving the way for structural change to happen; in creating structures which record these behaviours that discipline women, they are able to expose the unacceptability of it. This embedding of recognition into our state structures sends the signal that this is legally (and therefore morally) unacceptable. And it is this culture of *un*acceptance (refutation) of misogyny, and violence toward women, that our structures should be normalizing. This refutation needs to be what forms the basis of formal political structures, our media narratives, our organizational structures.

This example speaks to the collective capacity of our societal institutions and organizations to reverse and challenge sexism. While our structures may be responding to the demands of feminist activists and writers, and indeed, include feminist activists and writers, we might think of how we want to see not just representational shift but a reversal of neoliberal individualized cultural values. These cultural values can also be different. In 1974 Robin Morgan argued that sisterhood is powerful.[14] This was of course about the political power of women acting collectively, and also implied a different way of valuing women, and of seeing them. But there is also an implicit politics of care in that knowledge of collective support. Collectivity is something that has characterized feminist activism; the recognition of the strength of shared experiences and understanding as a driving force. But more than that, this collectivity is about looking after each other and looking out for each other. A shared understanding of oppression and exploitation that is located in caring for and about each other.

Empathy, perhaps, is one of the most fundamental features of a politically powerful feminism. As Ann Oakley argued, it allows for a different quality of understanding and knowledge.[15] I may be writing as a white woman, and may never truly understand what it is like to experience this world as a woman of colour. But I can try. And I can listen. As Peggy McIntosh argued, I can check my privilege.[16] I can 'unlearn' my privilege. For a diversity of women to be able to unite, and for men to be able to support, empathy is one of our key powerful unifying concepts, where we can listen to another to try and understand their perspective and adjust our own behaviour accordingly. Then we have a kinder, fairer, more compassionate place from which to express a feminist politics. Empathy invites us to hold on to a nuanced understanding of sisterhood, focused not on biology but on recognition of structural disadvantage. Empathy has long been part of the feminist agenda. For Patricia Hill Collins, empathy is foundational to African-American community formation.[17] It enables real conversations where knowledge claims can be understood on their own terms, rather than through their positioning in existing raced and sexist structures.

Reversal reinforces the notion that we do not have to accept our positioning as isolated neoliberal individuals in an invisible patriarchal structure. We can reverse sexism as individuals and as collectives and we can (and should) also expect and demand that our public institutions do the same. We can act collectively, and we can seek value change alongside changes in behaviour and numbers. A politics of empathy requires that speakers be heard, and that their testimonies provide the basis for a collective, active change for the better of all. bell hooks argues that feminism is for everyone.[18] So thinking about a feminism located in empathy and understanding is a way in which the values that we hold and cherish can help us reject our dominant patriarchal positioning.

Repoliticizing

To repoliticize sexism, we need to make it visible and expose the power structures that underlie, legitimate and perpetuate a system premised on the subordination of women. It is not just women who lose out in our contemporary systems of privilege and entitlement. Men who also do not fit comfortably with their own structural entitlement can also be disadvantaged. Calling out the patriarchy and sexism requires huge structural change combined with and supported by cumulative moments of individual action. Just as women call out sexism when they see and experience it, maybe it is time for *all* men to call out the male *benefits* of patriarchy when they see it: that men can safely walk home alone after a night out without having to incur the expense of a taxi; that men do not have to avoid getting into lifts with other men if they are on their own; that men have uniforms that fit as a default position; that men do not need to carry handbags because the pockets in their clothes are big enough; that men can be promoted over and above their abilities ... and so on. Much as dismantling sexism requires women to do the work of identifying and exposing their exploitation and oppression, we might also require men to recognize and speak up about the ways in which they are beneficiaries of this system. For men to ask, 'how would a woman experience this?' means the recognition of the systemic privileges conferred because of their biological sex. This critical question is part of the process of unlearning, and in so doing becomes a component of the role and work of men in repoliticizing sexism.

To repoliticize and expose sexism, we need to understand how our patriarchal conversations are structured and how they take place. We need to do that at societal level, organizational level and individual level. We need to make explicit how structures work. #MeToo has highlighted yet again how solutions are presented to us as a neoliberal 'lean in' narrative of 'fix the woman'. But the women do not need fixing. It is the system that is broken, not the women. It is a system which defines the narrow expectations of what a woman looks like, and what it is possible for her to achieve. It is a system that makes women's contributions, for example to the economy, invisible in the way in which work is referred to as meaning paid work, which has historically meant men's work; women's unpaid domestic labour has not been part of a discourse of 'work'. Changing the conversation at societal level means making gendered power structures explicit. Let us see, for example, football campaigns not just designed to kick racism [against men] out of football, but to end sexual violence against women. Let us see media headlines expressing outrage that 'Asian women are the worst affected by austerity measures'. Let us see media front pages that say 'we need to talk about racism in our society, not blame societal problems on women wearing Burqas'.

Changing the conversation also means thinking about our privilege before we speak. What are we saying, who are we saying it to? And whose interests are we reflecting when we speak. Are we speaking from a position of white privilege? Of male privilege? Of middle-class privilege? This change of conversation is part of making the structures visible so that we can see them. For example, calling sexual violence 'male sexual violence against women', where that is what it is, and if it is male to male violence, calling it in such terms (or female to male, or female to female). If we rethought how we talked about violence, instead of hiding the ways in which men dominate violent acts and aggressions, we would make this visible. In making problems visible we are able to confront them. To undo sexism we need to be in control of the narrative, so that we can change it and not be defined by it. To do that we need to understand and unpack how that narrative has been structured. In making these structures visible we repoliticize sexism.

The women who gave testimony to their experiences of the sexual violation and assault of Black women by white men gave birth to the civil rights movement.[19] Their testimonies were extraordinarily powerful. They revealed a pattern of abuse and exploitation in raced and gendered terms and made structures that had oppressed and exploited them visible. Giving testimony provides the basis for collective action; through collective action narratives are reclaimed. This is a crucial political lesson. We do not have to accept the patriarchal myths and narratives that are imposed on us. We can recognize them as imposed structures, rather than as inevitable or natural. MeToo/#MeToo are examples of how rage, and those 'fuck you' moments, can be mobilized as collective movements.[20] But for this to be more than just a moment or another 'wave' in the narrative history of feminist histories, as Helen Wood so wonderfully says, 'we need to sort this fucking shit out'.[21]

Rose Gann argues that rather than see feminism in waves, we can conceptualize it as highlighting both utopia and dystopia.[22] In this sense, much like the concept of respair, we can illustrate perhaps the utter awfulness of the impact of the structures of patriarchies upon women, but at the same time, recognize the opportunities that women [and men] can create, and imagine, and indeed achieve, alternative futures; like the peaks and troughs of a wave. The combination of utopia and dystopia reminds us that the history of feminism is fluid, offering emancipatory opportunities as well as cataloguing exploitation and oppression. Presenting the history of feminism as waves suggests linear progress. We break down one barrier, we are freed, and then we move to the next barrier. But as noted, the waves analogy, so dominant in the ways we talk about feminism per se, suggests peaks, but very little forward movement. Yes, we do see coastal erosion, and we can see some erosion of the patriarchal structures for women in the workplace. But the landscape has not really shifted. As has been noted in this book, it is still women who bear the brunt of poverty and violence in our world today. So perhaps we should be thinking about feminism as offering the opportunity for a tsunami. Tsunami's are linked to loss and fundamental devastation of society; maybe it is about time we talked about feminism as a tsunami that eradicates white masculinized structures of power, rather than a gradual shift in our seascape. Every 'fuck you' moment is another pent up bit of energy in the rumbling of the earthquake that can create a tsunami of 'fuck this'. Each exposure of and challenge to sexism is a political act; from individual stances and harnessing of rage to collective creativity we can challenge the very foundations of a societal system premised upon advancing the interests of entitled men.

From #MeToo to the politics of change

What has been argued in this book is that focusing on individual women's experiences as isolated moments serves to ignore the politics that underpin sexism. The history of feminist theorizing and activism has often been marginalized in our mediated narratives. #MeToo (and the subsequent Time's Up! campaign) have been presented to us as 'moments' rather than something with historical foregrounding. #MeToo has also been discussed in absence of the conditions that underpin it. To understand the possibilities for change we need to understand the complex ways in which sexism is deeply embedded in our social and cultural structures. In this book, I have reflected on just some of the ways in which sexism and misogyny are integrated into our belief systems and our media and political structures. Those belief systems rest on neoliberal assumptions of merit, intertwined with historically located systems which inflict violence on women through their disciplining and silencing. These levels of unseen but structural violence form the basis through which physical violence is legitimated and normalized.

Learning the lessons from #MeToo, I suggest, means that we need to move from the individual expression and moment in #MeToo, to the politics of change that can dismantle the patriarchy and patriarchies. MeToo/#MeToo as wider phenomena can be illustrative of an era that we are in, and an era that can be changed; we have been provided opportunities to repoliticize sexism. The collective voice of women's abuse has challenged our dominant mediated narratives. For some it has come as a shock that women have these experiences; for others the experiences are all too familiar. We are in danger of depoliticizing this moment if we ignore the histories of those who have gone before and the celebration of what women have already collectively achieved together. The stories that we tell about our feminist history matter.[23] We need also to learn the lessons from the past; what feminist activists have repeatedly learned is that the sand shifts beneath our feet, the pressure releases after each gain, but then patriarchy reinvents itself. If we write the history of women's stories out of our understandings and analysis of the MeToo/#MeToo phenomena, we are in danger of continuing to discipline and silence women and their achievements.

#MeToo needs to be more than just the next wave; we have to fundamentally undo the sexist structures that bind. We need a tsunami of feminism for this period in time not to be designated another wave. What #MeToo has invited us to do, as with the history of feminist theorizing beforehand, is to ask, what were the conditions that have led to the experiences of these women in the first place? And how do we undo those systems and structures of sexism? What I have argued here is that a depoliticization of sexism and misogyny has occurred through our neoliberal, individualized, mediated culture. Women are still being judged by masculinized standards and rules of the game. In this sense, women may never be seen as 'good enough' to compete with white entitled men who set the agenda and game rules, because they are not white entitled men.

This is not only through the under-representation of women in our public lives, in media and in politics, but it is in the way our white Westernized cultural narrative is constructed. In this neoliberal context, the focus is on the woman as the problem when she speaks out. As Sara Ahmed notes, all too often 'to name the problem is to be positioned as the problem'.[24] In refusing to address the problems that women raise as they navigate patriarchal environments, and identifying the woman who raises the problem as *the* problem, we make these patriarchal norms and values invisible. This invisibility of women and their interests takes place all around us where women are expected to behave according to masculinized definitions of femininity, which require them to bear the costs of male economic development; where women are disciplined and silenced in the advancement of male interests; and where women are punished, through threats and reality of male violence when they transgress these norms. What I have wanted to draw out here, however, is that it is not the woman who is the problem, but the system. A system that is in need of dramatic ethical change and reform.

While #MeToo has captured rage and anger at women's treatment and experiences at the hands of men and the patriarchy, it has been characterized, I would suggest, by two other crucial features. The first is utter despair, that things may not change and that we will have this moment and then be back to sexism as usual. At the same time, the anger for and by women is silenced, delegitimized and disallowed. So in this sense, anger is an important feature to recognize, in both the embedding of sexism and in the possibility of its undoing. Because it leads us to the second aspect: rage. This is what we need to maintain as the more powerful component; the sense that things could be different, better in a system premised not in violence but in empathy.

Appendix: Practical Steps to Overcoming Cultural Sexism

As I have noted this is not just an academic book but a personal book too. I have been in a position where I am not only writing about the sexism that characterizes our media culture, but the consequences of experiencing it in my everyday life (as most women I know also do). There is a link between what our mediated culture tells us the world looks like and the everyday experiences of women; just because we have not quantified this, does not mean it does not exist.

Here are just some of the things that I have been reminded of over the years as I have learned how to respond to and navigate the culture that we are situated in.

- If you are a women and are assaulted, harassed, abused or subjected to any form of sexism, it is not your fault.
- Do tell someone what has happened. That could be a friend, a colleague, a family member, a member of staff. But tell someone that you trust. It is a huge first step to speak about what has happened. Telling someone you trust is probably the biggest first step in processing what is happening/has happened to you.
- Build a support network around you of friends, family and colleagues. People that you trust and you know you can rely on to support you.
- Call it out. We do not have to put up with this, call it out when it happens to you, or others.
- If this is at work, talk to people in senior positions who can help. But if you are not getting the help you want or need, look elsewhere. It is out there and it is exhausting having these battles with people who do not understand your experience.

- Remember, there is a 'sisterhood' out there, at the very least, we see it every time we make eye contact with a woman on the street and smile at her.
- If you are experiencing any form of sexism, remember that being in this position is exhausting. Pick your battles as you cannot take them all on.
- It is okay to have a 'feminist day off'!
- There are good men out there who are also willing to support. And you may find them in the most unexpected of places.
- Equally, sadly, sometimes we have to remind men it is not okay to harass, abuse, gaslight, undermine and belittle women.

I have been immensely inspired by some wonderful people around me. It is with their kindness and support that we have been able to work towards changing our world in the following ways:

- We have created a women's network with the explicit aim of providing a safe space for women in our organization to feel they are supported and can talk.
- We have written to our management in a constructive bid to address the gender pay gap and support the advancement of women across the organization.
- I have understood the importance of reaching out and asking for help as well as seeking to provide it.
- I am working with my female students to improve their confidence and rejection of raced and sexist mediated messages that surround them. This has probably been one of the most pleasurable aspects of this whole experience.

I am lucky that I am in a workspace where this is possible and recognize that not everyone might be. Moreover, these are issues that do not only happen at work, but are part of our wider mediated culture. And so the same guidance and support as previously mentioned:

- You are not alone.
- It is okay to be angry.
- Talk to other people, male or female, there is always someone who will 'get it'.

- Read some of (or all of!) the feminist literature. A wonderful starting point is Sara Ahmed's *Living a Feminist Life*.
- Do not internalize the sexism that surrounds you.
- Affirm every day what you are capable of.

Acknowledgements

In the late 1950s, my mum gained a good honours undergraduate degree in English and a research degree at a Russell Group university. Upon leaving she applied for job after job, and was met with the same response each time: 'we don't employ women in executive positions'. I am lucky that I am in a position where because of the women who have fought for women's rights, I am able to hold a position in a university and to have the space and support to write this book.

So we may think that things have changed for women. Relentless headlines and media discourses tell us that women can 'have it all'; suggesting women can work *and* be responsible for childcare and home. Lucky them. Yet we do not see those headlines proclaiming that men can now 'have it all'. Because this statement does not need making. The system we live in has been constructed in the interests and for the benefit of men. They had it all already.

This sense of masculinized entitlement and assumed expectation of 'having it all', I think, is how we have found ourselves in the position of the widespread abuse, assault and harassment of women that #MeToo has drawn our attention to, alongside a history of sexism, abuse and violence underpinning our political and social systems.

It was a conversation with Stephen Wenham, Publisher at Bristol University Press, that began this project. He reminded me that actually it is okay to be angry about this, and maybe I'd like to write about it. So I would like to start by thanking him for his enthusiasm for the project, his intellectual critical engagement, support and humour along the way. His consistent support throughout and fantastic editorial skills, have been what has made this book possible. My thanks also go to Caroline

Astley and Vaarunika Dharmapala at Bristol University Press, and my copy-editor Michele Toler, for their kindness and professionalism, and care that they have shown around this work. I would also like to thank the anonymous reviewers who have engaged throughout the process. I hope I have done justice to your constructive, insightful and thoughtful comments.

I have been lucky to have some wonderful colleagues at De Montfort University (DMU). Justin Smith (where is my bag??!), thank you for being my critical friend, in so many senses of the word. Thank you also for the support, the ideas and the way in which you have engaged with this book. Simon Mills (Dylan) and Paul Smith (Zebedee) — you have been central in helping me make sense of my job, providing support and encouragement, with a healthy dose of realism and social justice. Thank you. Thank you also to Chris Hall for the laughs and the support.

I have been hugely inspired by the women around me at DMU. I would especially like to thank the Women Profs at DMU. I hope you have some idea just how much you have helped me retain my sanity! Kenetta Hammond-Perry, Jackie Labbe, Lala Meredith-Vula, Bertha Ochieng, Jo Richardson, Liz Tingle, Sarah Younie, YAY for finding you all and having you in my life, you are truly wonderful friends and inspiring role models. To Bally Dhalu, for being there, and getting it. Thank you. Vicky Ball, Shardia Briscoe-Palmer, Julia Havas, Rosey Hill, Jilly Kay, Indrani Lahiri, Ulrike Kubatta, Kaity Mendes, Ellen Wright for our lovely friendships and for reading, supporting and for sharing the rage.

My awesome inquisitive students who have reminded me of the fun we can have when we are being 'political'. In particular Sulei, Marvellous, Brittney, Keeley, Lydia, Anika, Jennifer, Becca, Serena, Maryam, Dorothy, Andrea, Karolina and all of my fab third year 'girl power' students: *always* remember that you rock. Jenny Alexander for being wonderful you. Karen Boyle, for listening, believing and guiding. Thank you. Sara Crabtree and all at the Women's Academic Network in Bournemouth, for all of your energy and support. Rose Gann thank you for reaching out, and for being there. Richard Scullion for being that continued source of wisdom, kindness and inspirational friendship. Helen Wood, thank you for being a wonderful inspiration, as both a scholar and a friend. And of course, we have Jaeger. Dominic Wring, an immense thank you for your continued kindness, sagacity and support. Candy Yates for being my funny, generous role model and sensible friend!

To my very dear friends outside of the academy who have also taken time to engage and provide feedback on this project: my dearest Thea Hinde. You have kept me sane, made me laugh and reminded me that it doesn't have to be like this. I'll send you a postcard when we get there (and we will). To Ken, Horst and Cara, Martin and Jackie, Matt and Thom, Bob and Mark. Your support and engagement has been immense. To the Maiden Adventure, and Shannon. You have made me laugh so much and been part of some of the funniest and most 'normal' (and therefore brilliant) times of my life.

You are all what a feminist looks like.

To my family. Hazel, thank you for your careful comments on an earlier draft. Thanks also for making me laugh in those moments where it *may* just have been possible that I lost my sense of humour ☺, and for keeping a tally on all my comedy accidents. Thanks to my mum for supporting and encouraging my academic endeavours and for loving my husband. Ann and Pat, Sarah and Shaun, David and Danielle, for the love and kindness you have shown welcoming me into your family.

Sam – we are all so proud of you. Your ways of thinking and making sense of the world are really powerful; you have a great future ahead of you. Krissy – you are such an inspirational trailblazer. It is wonderful to have you in our lives. Simon, thank you for helping me see how I could channel my rage creatively, and for catching me when I have been falling. And, of course, for Iron Maiden, Rammstein and Elvis.

Copyright acknowledgements

Sections in Chapter 4 originally published in Evans, E. Ahrens, P. Celis, K. Childs, S., Engeli, I. and Mügge, L. (eds) (2019) *European Journal of Politics and Gender*, 2(3): 363–79. Republished with the permission of Bristol University Press.

Notes

Introduction

1   Kantor, J. and Twohey, M. (2017) 'Harvey Weinstein paid off sexual harassment accusers for decades', *The New York Times*, 5 October [Online]. Available at https://www.nytimes.com/2017/10/05/us/harvey-weinstein-harassment-allegations.html (Accessed 6 November 2019); see also: Kantor, J. and Twohey, M. (2019) *She Said*, London: Bloomsbury.

2   France, L.R. (2017) '#MeToo: Social media flooded with personal stories of assault', *CNN*, 16 October [Online]. Available at https://edition.cnn.com/2017/10/15/entertainment/me-too-twitter-alyssa-milano/index.html (Accessed 6/11/2019).

3   Perraudin, F. (2019) '#MeToo two years on: Weinstein allegations "tip of iceberg" say accusers', *The Guardian*, 14 October [Online]. Available at https://www.theguardian.com/world/2019/oct/14/metoo-two-years-weinstein-allegations-tip-of-iceberg-accusers-zelda-perkins-rosanna-arquette (Accessed 15/10/19).

4   My focus is on Western media, predominantly US and UK. This has been challenging, as while I do not wish to reinforce the centrality of Western dominance and cultural imperialism, nonetheless I want to offer a critique of that centrality, and in so doing this means the examples that I use are drawn largely from the US and UK.

5   Hirsch, A. (2018) *Brit(ish): On Race, Identity and Belonging*, London: Random House; Zephaniah, B. (2019) *The Life and Rhymes of Benjamin Zephaniah: The Autobiography*, Scribner UK; Eddo-Lodge, R. (2017) *Why I'm No Longer Talking to White People about Race*, London: Bloomsbury Circus; Akala (2019) *Natives: Race and Class in the Ruins of Empire*, London: Two Roads.

6   Spender, D. (1982) *Women of Ideas and What Men Have Done to Them: From Aphra Behn to Adrienne Rich*, London and Boston: Routledge & Kegan Paul.

7   Boyle, K. (2019) *#MeToo, Weinstein & Feminism*, London: Palgrave Macmillan.

8   Spender, D. (1982) *Women of Ideas and What Men Have Done to Them: From Aphra Behn to Adrienne Rich*, London and Boston: Routledge & Kegan Paul, pp 32–42.

9   Wollstonecraft, M. (2015) *A Vindication of the Rights of Woman*, London: Vintage (1792), Ch IV.

10 Jex-Blake, S. (1886) *Medical Women: A Thesis and a History*, Edinburgh: Oliphant, Anderson & Ferrier.

11 Burstyn, J.N. (1973) 'Education and sex: the medical case against higher education for women in England, 1870-1900', *Proceedings of the American Philosophical Society*, 117(2): 79–89.

12 Goldman, E. (1910/2005) *Anarchism and Other Essays*, New York: Cosimo Inc.

13 Weinman Lear, M. (1968) 'The second feminist wave', *The New York Times Magazine*, 10 March.

14 Firestone, S. (1970/2015) *The Dialectic of Sex*, London: Verso.

15 de Beauvoir, S. (1949/1997) *The Second Sex*, London: Verso.

16 MacKinnon, C.A. (1979) *Sexual Harassment of Working Women: A Case of Sex Discrimination*, New Haven: Yale University Press; Dworkin, A. (1981) *Pornography: Men Possessing Women*, London: Women's Press.

17 Reagan, L.J. (2008) *When Abortion Was a Crime: Women, Medicine, and Law in the United States, 1867–1973*, Berkeley, Cal.: University of California Press.

18 Painter, N.I. (1996) *Sojourner Truth: A Life, a Symbol*, New York: W.W. Norton & Company, pp 164–74.

19 Woolf, V. (1931) *A Room of One's Own*, London: Hogarth Press, p 43.

20 Connell, R. (1995) *Masculinities*, Berkeley: University of California Press.

21 de Beauvoir, S. (1949/1997) *The Second Sex*, London: Verso; hooks, b. (1982) *Ain't I a Woman: Black Women and Feminism*, Boston, Mass.

22 Carrigan, T., Connell, B. and Lee, J. (1985) 'Toward a new sociology of masculinity', *Theory and Society*, 14(5): 551–604.

23 Carrigan, T., Connell, B. and Lee, J. (1985) 'Toward a new sociology of masculinity', *Theory and Society*, 14(5): 551–604.

24 Gill, R. (2009) 'Beyond the "sexualization of culture" thesis: an intersectional analysis of "Sixpacks", "Midriffs" and "Hot Lesbians" in Advertising', *Sexualities*, 12(2): 137–60; Mulvey, L. (1975) 'Visual pleasure and narrative cinema', *Screen*, 16(3): 6–18.

25 Projansky, S. (2001) *Watching Rape: Film and Television in Postfeminist Culture*, New York: New York University Press.

26 Practice, Advertising Standards Authority, Committee of Advertising (2017) *Depictions, Perceptions and Harm*, 18 July [Online]. Available at https://www.asa. org.uk/resource/depictions-perceptions-and-harm.html (Accessed 27 May 2019). For an example of the response see Mitchell, D. (2017) 'Sexism in advertising is a problem – but hardly the worst one', *The Guardian*, 23 July [Online]. Available at https://www.theguardian.com/commentisfree/2017/jul/23/exism-in-advertising-is-problem-but-hardly-worst-one-david-mitchell-asa-gender (Accessed 26 May 2019).

27 Bates, L. (2014) *Everyday Sexism*, London: Simon & Schuster; Bates, L. (2018) *Misogynation*, London: Simon & Schuster.

28 World Health Organization (2017) 'Violence against women', *World Health Organization*, 29 November [Online]. Available at https://www.who.int/news-room/fact-sheets/detail/violence-against-women (Accessed 26 May 2019).

29 Ingala Smith, K. (2013) 'Counting dead women', *Karen Ingala Smith* [Online]. Available at https://kareningalasmith.com/counting-dead-women/ (Accessed 24 May 2019).

Chapter 1

1 Hay, C. (2002) *Political Analysis*, Basingstoke: Palgrave.

2 Burke, T. (2007) 'The Inception', *Just Be Inc* [Online]. Available at http://justbeinc. wixsite.com/justbeinc/the-me-too-movement-cmml (Accessed 29 Oct 2018).

3 McGuire, D.L. (2010) *At the Dark End of the Street: Black Women, Rape, and Resistance – A New History of the Civil Rights Movement from Rosa Parks to the Rise of Black Power*, New York: Knopf; hooks, b. (1982) *Ain't I a Woman: Black Women and Feminism*, Boston, Mass.: South End Press; Brownmiller, S. (1975) *Against Our Will*, New York: Simon & Schuster.

4 McGuire, D.L. (2010) *At the Dark End of the Street: Black Women, Rape, and Resistance – A New History of the Civil Rights Movement from Rosa Parks to the Rise of Black Power*, New York: Knopf, p xx.

5 Emejulu, A. (2018) 'On the problems and possibilities of feminist solidarity: the Women's March one year on', *IPPR Progressive Review*, 24(4): 267–73.

6 Boyle, K. (2005) *Media and Violence*, London: Sage.

7 Boyle, K. (2020) *#MeToo, Weinstein and Feminism*, London: Palgrave.

8 Mendes, K., Ringrose, J. and Keller, J. (2019) *Digital Feminist Activism: Girls and Women Fight Back against Rape Culture*, Oxford: Oxford University Press.

9 Hollaback! (2005) *Hollaback!* [Online]. Available at https://www.ihollaback.org/about/ https://www.ihollaback.org/about/ (Accessed 28 May 2019).

10 Everyday Sexism Project (2012) *Everyday Sexism Project* [Online]. Available at www.everydaysexism.com (Accessed 27 May 2019).

11 Board, T.E. (2018) 'Confirmed: Brett Kavanaugh Can't Be Trusted', *The New York Times*, 7 September [Online]. Available at https://www.nytimes.com/2018/09/07/opinion/editorials/brett-kavanaugh-confirmation-hearings.html (Accessed 25 May 2019).

12 *Today* (2017) BBC Radio 4, 1 November.

13 Sanderson, D. (2018) '#MeToo shuts out men, says Keira Knightley', *The Times*, 29 December [Online]. Available at https://www.thetimes.co.uk/article/metoo-shuts-out-men-says-keira-knightley-6cqn2skxw (Accessed 26 May 2019).

14 Astier, H. (2018) 'France's celebrity pushback against "MeToo"', *BBC News*, 14 January [Online]. Available at https://www.bbc.co.uk/news/world-europe-42643504 (Accessed 28 May 2019).

15 Safronova, V., (2018) 'Catherine Deneuve and others denounce the MeToo movement', *The New York Times*, 9 January [Online]. Available at https://www.nytimes.com/2018/01/09/movies/catherine-deneuve-and-others-denounce-the-metoo-movement.html (Accessed 11 Nov 2019).

16 Telegraph Reporters (2018) 'Catherine Deneuve signs letter denouncing #MeToo "witch hunt": "Men should be free to hit on women"', *The Telegraph*, 9 January [Online]. Available at https://www.telegraph.co.uk/films/2018/01/09/catherine-deneuve-signs-letter-denouncing-metoo-witch-hunt-men/ (Accessed 11 Nov 2019).

17 Le Monde Collective (2018) 'Full translation of French anti-#MeToo manifesto signed by Catherine Deneuve', *Worldcrunch*, 10 January [Online]. Available at https://www.worldcrunch.com/opinion-analysis/full-translation-of-french-anti-metoo-manifesto-signed-by-catherine-deneuve (Accessed 12 Nov 2019).

18 Jane, E.A. (2014) '"Your a ugly, whorish, slut"': understanding e-bile', *Feminist Media Studies*, 14(4): 1–16; Jane, E.A. (2015) 'Flaming? What flaming? The pitfalls and potentials of researching online hostility', *Ethics and Information Technology*, 17(1): 65–87.

19 Lumsden, K. and Morgan, H. (2017) 'Media framing of trolling and online abuse: silencing strategies, symbolic violence, and victim blaming', *Feminist Media Studies*, 17(6): 926–40; Citron, D.K. (2009) 'Law's expressive value in combating cyber gender harassment', *Michigan Law Review*, 108(3): 373–415.

20 Mantilla, K. (2015) *GenderTrolling: How Misogyny Went Viral*, California: ABC-CLIO, LLC.

21 Hanisch, C. (1970) 'The personal is political', in S. Firestone and A. Koedt (eds) *Notes from the Second Year: Women's Liberation*, PO Box AA: Old Chelsea Station, pp 76–7.

22   hooks, b. (1982) *Ain't I a Woman: Black Women and Feminism*, Boston, Mass.: South End Press; Crenshaw, K. (1991) 'Mapping the margins: intersectionality, identity politics, and violence against women of color', *Stanford Law Review*, 43(6): 1241–99; Lorde, A. (1984) *Sister Outsider: Essays and Speeches*, Trumansburg, NY: Crossing Press.

23   Enloe, C. (2000) *Bananas, Beaches and Bases: Making Feminist Sense of International Politics*, Berkeley Cal., London: University of California Press.

24   See for example Welsh, S., Carr, J., MacQuarrie, B. and Huntley, A. (2006) '"I'm not thinking of it as sexual harassment": understanding harassment across race and citizenship', *Gender & Society*, 20(1): 87–107; Dodd, E.H., Giuliano, T.A., Boutell, J.M. and Moran, B.E. (2001) 'Respected or rejected: perceptions of women who confront sexist remarks', *Sex Roles*, 45(7–8): 567–77; Hlavka, H.R. (2014) 'Normalizing sexual violence: young women account for harassment and abuse', *Gender & Society*, 28(3): 337–58; Rogers, J.K. and Henson, K.D. (1997) '"Hey, why don't you wear a shorter skirt?": structural vulnerability and the organization of sexual harassment in temporary clerical employment', *Gender & Society*, 11(2): 215–37; Fitzgerald, L.F., Swan, S. and Fischer, K. (1995) 'Why didn't she just report him? The psychological and legal implications of women's responses to sexual harassment', *Journal of Social Issues*, 51(1): 117–38.

25   Appignanesi, L. (2008) *Mad, Bad and Sad: Women and the Mind Doctors*, New York: W.W. Norton & Co.

26   A really useful anthology of these debates is provided in Harding, S. (ed) (2003) *The Feminist Standpoint Theory Reader: Intellectual and Political Controversies*, New York and London: Routledge.

27   Spivak, G.C., Landry, D. and MacLean, G.M. (1996) *The Spivak Reader: Selected Works of Gayatri Chakravorty Spivak*, Routledge, New York: London

28   Duncan, P., McIntyre, N. and Davies, C. (2019) 'Gender pay gap figures show eight in 10 UK firms pay men more than women', *The Guardian*, 4 April [Online]. Available at https://www.theguardian.com/world/2019/apr/04/gender-pay-gap-figures-show-eight-in-10-uk-firms-pay-men-more-than-women (Accessed 28 May 2019).

29   Enloe, C. (2013) *Seriously!: Investigating Crashes and Crises as if Women Mattered*, Berkeley, Cal.: University of California Press.

Chapter 2

1   Moradi, B. and Funderburk, J.R. (2006) 'Roles of perceived sexist events and perceived social support in the mental health of women seeking counseling', *Journal of Counseling Psychology*, 53(4): 464–73.

2   Shapiro, F.R. (1985) 'Historical notes on the vocabulary of the women's movement', *American Speech*, 60(1): 3–16.

3   Leet, P. (1965) 'Women and the undergraduate', *Mimeo*, p 3.

4   Leet, P. (1965) 'Women and the undergraduate', *Mimeo*, p 3.

5   *Time Magazine* (1998) 'Is feminism dead', *Time Magazine*, 29 June [Online]. Available at http://content.time.com/time/covers/0,16641,19980629,00.html (Accessed 19 November 2019).

6   Faludi, S. (1991) *Backlash: The Undeclared War against American Women*, New York: Doubleday.

7   Faludi, S. (1991) *Backlash: The Undeclared War against American Women*, New York: Doubleday.

8   Whelehan, I. (2000) *Overloaded: Popular Culture and the Future of Feminism*, London: Women's Press.

9   McRobbie, A. (2004) 'Post-feminism and popular culture', *Feminist Media Studies*, 4(3): 255–64.

10   Gill, R. (2007) 'PostFeminist media culture', *European Journal of Cultural Studies*, 10(2): 147–66.

11   Douglas, S.J. (2010) *Enlightened Sexism: The Seductive Message that Feminism's Work is Done*, New York: Times Books.

12   Banyard, K. (2010), *The Equality Illusion: The Truth about Women and Men Today*, London: Faber and Faber.

13   Crenshaw, K. (1989) 'Demarginalizing the intersection of race and sex: a black feminist critique of antidiscrimination doctrine, feminist theory and antiracist politics', *University of Chicago Legal Forum*, 1(8): 139–67.

14   hooks, b. (1982) *Ain't I a Woman: Black Women and Feminism*, Boston, Mass.; Hill Collins, P. (1990) *Black Feminist Thought: Knowledge, Consciousness, and the Politics of Empowerment*, New York and London: Routledge; Crenshaw, K. (1991) 'Mapping the margins: intersectionality, identity politics, and violence against women of color', *Stanford Law Review*, 43(6): 1241–99; Eddo-Lodge, R. (2017), *Why I'm No Longer Talking to White People about Race*, London: Bloomsbury Circus.

15   Ahmed, S. (2016) 'Losing confidence', *Feminist Killjoys*, 1 March [Blog]. Available at https://feministkilljoys.com/2016/03/01/losing-confidence/ (Accessed 7 January 2019).

16   Aristotle, Barker, E. and Stalley, R.F. (2009) *Politics*, Oxford and New York: Oxford University Press.

17   Rousseau, J. and Payne, W.H. (1893) *Rousseau's Emile*, London: Arnold.

18   For example, Engels, F. (1902) *The Origin of the Family, Private Property and the State*, Chicago: C.H. Kerr & Co.

19   Engels, F. (1902) *The Origin of the Family, Private Property and the State*, Chicago: C.H. Kerr & Co.

20   Engels, F. (1902) *The Origin of the Family, Private Property and the State*, Chicago: C.H. Kerr & Co., p 137.

21   Engels, F. (1902) *The Origin of the Family, Private Property and the State*, Chicago: C.H. Kerr & Co., p 120.

22   Firestone, S. (1970) *The Dialectic of Sex: The Case for Feminist Revolution*, London: Woman's Press.

23   Specia, M. (2018) 'How Savita Halappanavar's death spurred Ireland's abortion rights campaign', *The New York Times*, 27 May [Online]. Available at https://www.nytimes.com/2018/05/27/world/europe/savita-halappanavar-ireland-abortion.html (Accessed 1 June 2019).

24   Cosslett, R.L. (2017) 'This photo sums up Trump's assault on women's rights', *The Guardian*, 24 January [Online]. Available at https://www.theguardian.com/commentisfree/2017/jan/24/photo-trump-womens-rights-protest-reproductive-abortion-developing-contries (Accessed 1 June 2019).

25   Oppenheim, M. (2019) 'Roe vs Wade: abortion could be made illegal with Brett Kavanaugh on Supreme Court, says Michigan Attorney General', *The Independent*, 17 April [Online]. Available at https://www.independent.co.uk/news/world/americas/roe-v-wade-overturn-abortion-brett-kavanaugh-supreme-court-dana-nessel-michigan-a8874946.html (Accessed 19 November 2019).

26   Mead, M. (1949) *Male and Female: A Study of the Sexes in a Changing World*, New York: W. Morrow.

27   Millett, K. (1968) *Sexual Politics*, Boston, Mass.: New England Free Press.

28 Butler, J.P. (1990) *Gender Trouble: Feminism and the Subversion of Identity*, New York: Routledge.

29 Manne, K. (2018) *Down Girl: The Logic of Misogyny*, New York: Oxford University Press, p 33.

30 Manne, K. (2018) *Down Girl: The Logic of Misogyny*, New York: Oxford University Press, p 33.

31 Bailey, M. (2010) 'They aren't talking about me...', *Crunk Feminist Collective*, 14 March [Online]. Available at http://www.crunkfeministcollective.com/2010/03/14/they-arent-talking-about-me/ (Accessed 28 May 2019).

32 Taylor, J. (2018) 'The woman who founded the 'incel' movement', *BBC News*, 30 August [Online]. Available at https://www.bbc.co.uk/news/world-us-canada-45284455 (Accessed 19 November 2019).

33 Hendrix, S. (2019) 'He always hated women. Then he decided to kill them.' *Washington Post*, 7 June [Online]. Available at https://www.washingtonpost.com/graphics/2019/local/yoga-shooting-incel-attack-fueled-by-male-supremacy/ (Accessed 8 June 2019).

34 Kassam, A. (2018) 'Woman behind 'incel' says angry men hijacked her word "as a weapon of war"', *The Guardian*, 26 April [Online]. Available at https://www.theguardian.com/world/2018/apr/25/woman-who-invented-incel-movement-interview-toronto-attack (Accessed 27 May 2019).

35 Emba, C. (2019) 'Men are in trouble. "Incels" are proof', *Washington Post*, 7 June [Online]. Available at https://www.washingtonpost.com/opinions/men-are-in-trouble-incels-are-proof/2019/06/07/8d6ad596-8936-11e9-a870-b9c411dc4312_story.html (Accessed 8 June 2019).

36 Mulvey, L. (1975), 'Visual pleasure and narrative cinema', *Screen*, 16(3): 6–18.

37 Szymanski, D.M., Gupta, A., Carr, E.R. and Stewart, D. (2009) 'Internalized misogyny as a moderator of the link between sexist events and women's psychological distress', *Sex Roles*, 61(1–2): 101–9.

38 Ahmed, S. (2017) *Living a Feminist Life*, Durham: Duke University Press.

39 Morgan, R. (1973) *Sisterhood is Powerful*, Random House Inc: US.

40 hooks, b. (1982) *Ain't I a Woman: Black Women and Feminism*, Boston, Mass.; Lorde, A. (1984) *Sister Outsider: Essays and Speeches*, Trumansburg, NY: Crossing Press.

41 For example, Harding, S. (ed) (2003) *The Feminist Standpoint Theory Reader: Intellectual and Political Controversies*, New York and London: Routledge.

42 hooks, b. (2000) *Feminism is for Everybody: Passionate Politics*, London: Pluto; Eddo-Lodge, R. (2017) *Why I'm No Longer Talking to White People about Race*, London: Bloomsbury Circus.

43 Mendes, K., Ringrose, J. and Keller, J. (2019) *Digital Feminist Activism: Girls and Women Fight Back against Rape Culture*, Oxford and New York: Oxford University Press.

Chapter 3

1 Lee, J., Kim, S. and Ham, C.-D. (2016) 'A double-edged sword? Predicting consumers' attitudes toward and sharing intention of native advertising on social media', *American Behavioral Scientist*, 60(12): 1425–41.

2 Cadwalladr, C. (2018) 'The Cambridge Analytica Files. "I made Steve Bannon's psychological warfare tool": meet the data war whistleblower', *The Guardian*, 18 March [Online]. Available at http://davelevy.info/Downloads/cabridgeananalyticafiles%20-theguardian_20180318.pdf (Accessed 20 November 2019).

[3] Lewis, J. (2014) *Beyond Consumer Capitalism: Media and the Limits to Imagination*, Hoboken: Wiley.

[4] Crotty, M. (2018) *The Foundations of Social Research*, London: Sage.

[5] Reeves, A., McKee, M. and Stuckler, D. (2016) '"It's the Sun wot won it": evidence of media influence on political attitudes and voting from a UK quasi-natural experiment', *Social Science Research*, 56: 44–57.

[6] There are a range of tools that are now patented on Google to support this process, for example, Strutton, M.J., Delgado, P., Wilde, S.J., Estes, C., Turner, J., Schult John Maxwell, J., Reynolds, J.C., Pocius., B.S. II, Williams, H. and Nolt, J.B. (2019) 'Systems and methods for creating and inserting application media content into social media system displays', *Google Patents* [Online]. Available at https://patents.google.com/patent/US10339541B2/en (Accessed 20 November 2019).

[7] McCombs, M.E. and Shaw, D.L. (1972) 'The agenda-setting function of mass media', *The Public Opinion Quarterly*, 36(2): 177.

[8] Although for field changing exception see Griffin, E. (2013) *Liberty's Dawn: A People's History of the British Industrial Revolution*, Yale: Yale University Press.

[9] Hirsch, A. (2018) *Brit(ish): On Race, Identity and Belonging*, London: Jonathan Cape.

[10] Dekić, S., UN Women Europe and Central Asia (2017) *Media Coverage of Gender-Based Violence – Handbook and Training of Trainers* [Online]. Available at http://eca.unwomen.org/en/digital-library/publications/2017/09/media-coverage-of-gender-based-violence---handbook-and-training-of-trainers (Accessed 12 May 2019); D'Aprix, M. (2017) 'Women's stories we're missing as coverage of Trump dominates media', *Women's Media Center*, 20 June [Online]. Available at http://www.womensmediacenter.com/women-under-siege/womens-stories-were-missing-as-coverage-of-trump-dominates-media (Accessed 14 May 2019).

[11] Ingala Smith, K. (2013) 'Counting dead women', *Karen Ingala Smith* [Online]. Available at https://kareningalasmith.com/counting-dead-women/ (Accessed 16 May 2019).

[12] iTEAM (2019) 'Knife crime in the UK: list of the stabbing victims killed in 2019 so far, in London and beyond', *iNews*, 6 May [Online]. Available at https://inews.co.uk/news/uk/knife-crime-uk-2019-stabbing-victims-killed-full-list-london-statistics-502518 (Accessed 20 November 2019).

[13] Kitzinger, J. (2004) *Framing Abuse: Media Influence and Public Understanding of Sexual Violence against Children*, London: Pluto Press, p 31.

[14] Street, J. (2001) *Mass Media, Politics and Democracy*, Houndmills, Hampshire: Palgrave; Savigny, H. (2017) *Political Communication: A Critical Introduction*, London: Palgrave.

[15] Enloe, C. (2000) *Bananas, Beaches and Bases: Making Feminist Sense of International Politics*, Berkeley Cal., London: University of California Press.

[16] Smith, S.L., Choueiti, M. and Pieper, K. (2017) *Inequality in 900 Popular Films*, July [Online]. Available at https://annenberg.usc.edu/sites/default/files/Dr_Stacy_L_Smith-Inequality_in_900_Popular_Films.pdf (Accessed 15 May 2019).

[17] Mulvey, L. (1975), 'Visual pleasure and narrative cinema', *Screen*, 16(3): 6–18.

[18] Bechdel, A. (1986) *Dykes to Watch Out For*, Ithaca, N.Y.: Firebrand Books.

[19] *Bechdel Test Movie List* [Online]. Available at http://bechdeltest.com (Accessed 6 June 2019).

[20] Global Media Monitoring Project (2015) *Who Makes the News?* November [Online]. Available at http://cdn.agilitycms.com/who-makes-the-news/Imported/reports_2015/global/gmmp_global_report_en.pdf (Accessed 11 February 2019).

[21] Media Reform Coalition (2015) *Who Owns the UK Media?* [Online]. Available at https://www.mediareform.org.uk/wp-content/uploads/2015/10/Who_owns_the_UK_media-report_plus_appendix1.pdf (Accessed 12 February 2019).

22 Media Reform Coalition (2015) *Who Owns the UK Media?* [Online]. Available at https://www.mediareform.org.uk/wp-content/uploads/2015/10/Who_owns_the_UK_media-report_plus_appendix1.pdf (Accessed 12 February 2019).

23 Statista (2019) 'Distribution of Google employees worldwide from 2014 to 2018, by gender', *Statista,* April [Online]. Available at https://www.statista.com/statistics/311800/google-employee-gender-global/ (Accessed 29 January 2019).

24 Google (2018) *Google Diversity Annual Report* [Online]. Available at https://static.googleusercontent.com/media/diversity.google/en//static/pdf/Google_Diversity_annual_report_2018.pdf (Accessed 29 January 2019).

25 Statista (2019) 'Percentage of households with mobile phones in the United Kingdom (UK) from 1996 to 2018', *Statista,* January [Online]. Available at https://www.statista.com/statistics/289167/mobile-phone-penetration-in-the-uk/ (Accessed 22 November 2019).

26 Devlin, H. and Hern, A. (2017) 'Why are there so few women in tech? The truth behind the Google memo', *The Guardian,* 8 August [Online]. Available at https://www.theguardian.com/lifeandstyle/2017/aug/08/why-are-there-so-few-women-in-tech-the-truth-behind-the-google-memo (Accessed 14 January 2019).

27 O'Neill, H. (2018) 'Hyenas in petticoats and the man in a dress: women and the vote', *The London Library,* 8 February [Blog]. Available at http://blog.londonlibrary.co.uk/?p=17765

28 Gordon, C. (2015) *Romantic Outlaws: The Extraordinary Lives of Mary Wollstonecraft and Her Daughter Mary Shelley,* New York: Random House.

29 Gordon, C. (2015) *Romantic Outlaws: The Extraordinary Lives of Mary Wollstonecraft and Her Daughter Mary Shelley,* New York: Random House.

30 (1910) 'Saving women from suffragettes', *Manchester Evening News,* 3 November [Online]. Available at https://news.google.com/newspapers?nid=1790&dat=19101103&id=FJY9AAAAIBAJ&sjid=tisMAAAAIBAJ&pg=857,9095287 (Accessed 12 February 2019).

31 (1910) 'Violent scenes at Westminster where many suffragettes were arrested while trying to force their way into the House of Commons', *Daily Mirror,* 19 November [Online]. Available at https://commons.wikimedia.org/wiki/File:The_Daily_Mirror,_19_November_1910,_front_page_(cleaned).png (Accessed 12 February 2019).

32 Riddell, F. (2018) 'The 1910s: we have sanitised our history of the suffragettes', *The Guardian,* 6 February [Online]. Available at https://www.theguardian.com/lifeandstyle/2018/feb/06/1910s-suffragettes-suffragists-fern-riddell (Accessed 13 January 2019).

33 Faludi, S. (1991) *Backlash: The Undeclared War against American Women,* New York: Doubleday.

34 Orr, D. (2003) 'Who would want to call herself a feminist?' *The Independent,* 4 July [Online]. Available at https://www.independent.co.uk/voices/commentators/deborah-orr/who-would-want-to-call-herself-a-feminist-94623.html (Accessed 4 April 2019).

35 Baumgardner, J. and Richards, A. (2000) *Manifesta: Young Women, Feminism, and the Future,* New York: Farrar, Strauss and Giroux; Redfern, C. and Aune, K. (2013) *Reclaiming the F Word: Feminism Today,* London and New York: Zed Books.

36 Mendes, K. (2011) *Feminism in the News: Representations of the Women's Movement Since the 1960s,* Houndmills, Basingstoke, Hampshire; New York: Palgrave Macmillan.

37 Gill, R. and Scharff, C. (2011) *New Femininities – Postfeminism, Neoliberalism and Subjectivity,* Basingstoke: Palgrave.

38 Goldman, E. (1987) *Living My Life,* London: Pluto Press.

[39] Countess Constance Markievicz was also elected but, as a Sinn Fein MP, did not take her seat at Westminster.

[40] McGaffin, W. (1939) 'Lady Astor gets the spotlight but her viscount planned it that way', *The London Evening Day*, 16 August.

[41] Browning, S. (2019) 'Women in parliament and government', House of Commons Library, Number 01250, 4 March.

[42] British Library (2017) 'Blair's Babes', *Sound and Vision Blog*, 2 May [Online]. Available at https://blogs.bl.uk/sound-and-vision/2017/05/blairs-babes.html (Accessed 12 January 2019).

[43] Cooke, R. (2007), Oh babe, just look at us now', *The Guardian*, 22 April [Online]. Available at https://www.theguardian.com/politics/2007/apr/22/women.labour1 (Accessed 3 May 2018).

[44] de Beauvoir, S. (1949) *The Second Sex*, Harmondsworth, Middlesex, UK: Penguin Books.

[45] Prasad, R., (2018) 'Serena Williams and the trope of the "angry black woman"' *BBC News*, 11 September [Online]. Available at https://www.bbc.co.uk/news/world-us-canada-45476500 (Accessed 3 March 2019).

[46] Henderson, P. (2019) 'John McEnroe: "I'm still the guy that's paid not to be calm"', *GQ Magazine*, 29 June [Online]. Available at https://www.gq-magazine.co.uk/article/john-mcenroe-interview (Accessed 21 November 2019).

[47] Spivak, G.C. (1988) *Can the Subaltern Speak?* Basingstoke: Macmillan, p 287.

[48] Ward, O. (2017) 'Intersectionality and press coverage of political campaigns', *The International Journal of Press/Politics*, 22(1): 43–66.

[49] Wahl-Jorgensen, K. and Garcia-Blanco, I. (2012) 'The discursive construction of women politicians in the European press', *Feminist Media Studies*, 12(3): 422–41.

[50] O'Neill, D., Savigny, H. and Cann, V. (2016) 'Women politicians in the UK press: not seen and not heard?' *Feminist Media Studies*, 16(2): 293–307.

[51] Braden, M. (1996) *Women Politicians and the Media*, Lexington: University Press of Kentucky, p 8.

[52] Mulvey, L. (1975), 'Visual pleasure and narrative cinema', *Screen*, 16(3): 6–18.

[53] For excellent satirical discussion of this see Freeman, H. (2014) 'Oh yes. This is what Theresa May went into politics for', *The Guardian*, 18 July [Online]. Available at https://www.theguardian.com/commentisfree/2014/jul/18/theresa-politics-hot-spectator (Accessed 12 April 2019).

[54] Malkin, B. (2017) 'Daily Mail 'Legs-it' front page criticised as "sexist, offensive and moronic"', *The Guardian*, 28 March [Online]. Available at https://www.theguardian.com/media/2017/mar/28/daily-mail-legs-it-front-page-sexist (Accessed 3 April 2019).

[55] Falk, E. (2008) *Women for President: Media Bias in Nine Campaigns*, Chicago: University of Illinois Press, p 37.

[56] Harmer, E., Savigny, H. and Ward, O. (2017) '"Are you tough enough?" Performing gender in the UK leadership debates 2015', *Media, Culture & Society*, 39(7): 960–75.

[57] McKinstry, L. (2015) 'Stumbling Miliband is real loser', *Daily Express*, 3 April, p 5.

[58] Shipman, T. and Wheeler, C. (2018) 'Four meetings and a political funeral', *The Sunday Times*, 21 October [Online]. Available at https://www.thetimes.co.uk/article/four-meetings-and-a-political-funeral-n2079bn3v (Accessed 3 April 2019).

[59] Elgot, J. and Walker, P. (2018) 'Calls to remove Tory whip after "disgraceful" remarks about May', *The Guardian*, 22 October [Online]. Available at https://www.theguardian.com/politics/2018/oct/22/tories-identify-mps-vile-language-theresa-may-yvette-cooper (Accessed 28 January 2019).

60 Dhrodia, A. (2018) 'Unsocial media: a toxic place for women', *IPPR Progressive Review*, 24(4): 380–7.
61 Childs, S. (2010) *Women and British Party Politics: Descriptive, Substantive and Symbolic Representation*, London: Routledge.

Chapter 4

1 Hotten, R. (2018) 'All the good women have been snapped up', *BBC News*, 31 May [Online]. Available at https://www.bbc.co.uk/news/business-44310225 (Accessed 23 May 2019).
2 Young, M. (1958) *The Rise of the Meritocracy 1870–2033: An Essay on Education and Equality*, Hardmondsworth; New York: Penguin Books.
3 For an overview of the historical usage of the term see Iggers, G.G. (1993) 'Rationality and history', in H. Kozicki (ed) *Developments in Modern Historiography*, London: Palgrave Macmillan.
4 Farrall, S. and Hay, C. (2014) *The Legacy of Thatcherism: Assessing and Exploring Thatcherite Social and Economic Policies*, Oxford and New York: Oxford University Press.
5 Smith, A. (1776/1961) *An Inquiry into the Nature and Causes of the Wealth of Nations*, London: Methuen; von Hayek, F. (1944/2001) *The Road to Serfdom*, London: Routledge; Friedman, M. (1962/2002) *Capitalism and Freedom*, Chicago: University of Chicago Press.
6 Smith, A. (1776/1961) *An Inquiry into the Nature and Causes of the Wealth of Nations*, London: Methuen.
7 Klein, N. (2007) *The Shock Doctrine: The Rise of Disaster Capitalism*, New York: Metropolitan Books/Henry Holt.
8 Yates, C. (2019) '"Show us you care!" The gendered psycho-politics of emotion and women as political leaders', *European Journal of Politics & Gender*, 2(3): 345–61.
9 Golding, P. (1982) *Images of Welfare: Press and Public Attitude to Poverty*, London: Wiley-Blackwell.
10 Living Wage Foundation (2017) 'Women continue to be hardest hit by low wages in the UK', *Living Wage Foundation*, 10 November [Online]. Available at https://www.livingwage.org.uk/news/news-women-continue-be-hit-hardest-low-wages-uk (Accessed 22 May 2019).
11 As termed by Gaye Tuchman, in Tuchman, G., Daniels, A.K. and Benét, J. (1978) *Hearth and Home: Images of Women in the Mass Media*, New York: Oxford University Press.
12 Littler, J. (2018) *Against Meritocracy: Culture, Power and Myths of Mobility*, Abingdon, Oxon and New York: Routledge.
13 Wheen, F. (2001) 'Satirical fiction is becoming Blair's reality', *The Guardian*, 14 February [Online]. Available at https://www.theguardian.com/theguardian/2001/feb/14/features11.g21 (Accessed 22 May 2019).
14 Wilkinson, R.G. and Pickett, K. (2010) The spirit level: why greater equality makes societies stronger, Bloomsbury Press, New York.
15 Dorling, D. (2015) *Injustice: Why Social Inequality Still Persists*, Bristol: Policy Press.
16 Keegan, V. (1998) 'Economics notebook: raising the risk stakes', *The Guardian*, 26 October [Online]. Available at https://www.theguardian.com/Columnists/Column/0,,325036,00.html (Accessed 2 February 2019).
17 The Sunday Times (2019) 'The rich list', *The Sunday Times* [Online]. Available at https://www.thetimes.co.uk/article/sunday-times-rich-list-cbxfbprqf (Accessed 15 June 2019).

18 Enloe, C. (2013) *Seriously!: Investigating Crashes and Crises as if Women Mattered*, Berkeley, Cal.: University of California Press.

19 Fairclough, N. and Fairclough, I. (2012) *Political Discourse Analysis*, New York: Routledge, pp 135–8.

20 Hampton-Alexander Review FTSE Women Leaders (2018) *FTSE Women Leaders* [Online]. Available at https://ftsewomenleaders.com/ (Accessed 22 May 2019).

21 Noland, M. and Moran, T. (2016) *Study: Firms with More Women in the C-Suite Are More Profitable*, Peterson Institute for International Economics (PIIE), 8 February [Online]. Available at https://piie.com/commentary/op-eds/study-firms-more-women-c-suite-are-more-profitable (Accessed 15 June 2019).

22 Credit Suisse (2018) *Global Wealth Report 2018* [Online]. Available at https://www.credit-suisse.com/corporate/en/research/research-institute/global-wealth-report.html (Accessed 1 May 2019).

23 Elson, D. and Women's Budget Group (2018) *The Impact of Austerity on Women*; Women's Budget Group and Runnymede Trust (2018) *Intersecting Inequalities: The Impact of Austerity on Black and Minority Ethnic Women in the UK* [Online]. Available at http://wbg.org.uk/wp-content/uploads/2018/08/Intersecting-Inequalities-October-2017-Full-Report.pdf (Accessed 1 May 2019); see also Hall, S.M. (2018) 'The personal is political: feminist geographies of/in austerity', *Geoforum*, 16 April [Online]. Available at http://www.sciencedirect.com/science/article/pii/S0016718518301192 (Accessed 16 June 2019).

24 Elson, D. and Women's Budget Group (2018) *The Impact of Austerity on Women*.

25 All Party Parliamentary Group (2018) *All-Party Parliamentary Group on Sexual Violence Report into the Funding and Commissioning of Sexual Violence and Abuse Services 2018* [Online]. Available at https://rapecrisis.org.uk/media/1920/report-on-funding-and-commissioning-of-sv-and-abuse-services-2018.pdf (Accessed 23 May 2019).

26 Women's Grid (2018) 'A Crisis in Rape Crisis – Rape Crisis England and Wales', *Women's Grid*, 17 July [Online]. Available at https://www.womensgrid.org.uk/?p=6866 (Accessed 22 May 2019).

27 Rubery, J. (2015) 'Austerity, the public sector and the threat to gender equality', *The Economic and Social Review*, 46(1): 7.

28 Abramovitz, M. (2012) 'The feminization of austerity', *New Labor Forum*, January.

29 Stewart, H. and Syal, R. (2011) 'Jobless rate for young women doubles as council cuts start to bite', *The Guardian*, 13 February [Online]. Available at https://www.theguardian.com/uk/2011/feb/13/jobless-women-numbers-double (Accessed 13 March 2019).

30 House of Commons Women and Equalities Committee (2016) *Equalities analysis and the 2015 Spending Review and Autumn Statement*, 16 November [Online]. Available at https://publications.parliament.uk/pa/cm201617/cmselect/cmwomeq/825/825.pdf (Accessed 23 March 2019).

31 Cooper, V. and Whyte, D. (2017) *The Violence of Austerity*, London: Pluto Press.

32 Riches, C. (2018) 'Woman, 20, has throat slashed in hotel horror', *Daily Express*, 24 July [Online]. Available at https://www.express.co.uk/news/uk/993253/stabbing-throat-slash-woman-manchester-hilton-hotel (Accessed 4 April 2019).

33 Boyle, K. (2005) *Media and Violence*, London: Sage.

34 Newton Dunn, T. and Schofield, K. (2015) 'The Osborne Supremacy; £9 an hr living wage helps poor; £13bn is slashed off welfare bill', *The Sun*, 9 July, pp 4–5.

35 Gurdgiev, C. (2009) 'Slash public services, don't snip at the edges', *The Sunday Times*, 5 July, p 4.

36 Paul, M. (2009) 'Horror Story; The private sector is held up as a model to public-sector staff facing pay cuts. But, as Mark Paul discovers, the truth is employers are

taking a faster and bloodier route to chopping wage bills', *The Sunday Times*, 29 November, p 7.

37 Griffin, P. (2015) 'Crisis, austerity and gendered governance: a feminist perspective', *Feminist Review*, 109: 49–72.

38 See the TUC archives for further details of this and other equal pay victories, Trades Union Congress (2007) *TUC Equal Pay Archive* [Online]. Available at https://www.tuc.org.uk/publications/tuc-equal-pay-archive (Accessed 23 March 2019).

39 Furness, H. (2019) 'Female BBC manager turns down job claiming man in same role was offered £12,000 more', *The Telegraph*, 22 May [Online]. Available at https://www.telegraph.co.uk/news/2019/05/22/female-bbc-manager-turns-job-claiming-man-role-offered-12000/ (Accessed 30 May 2019).

40 Furness, H. (2019) 'Female BBC manager turns down job claiming man in same role was offered £12,000 more', *The Telegraph*, 22 May [Online]. Available at https://www.telegraph.co.uk/news/2019/05/22/female-bbc-manager-turns-job-claiming-man-role-offered-12000/ (Accessed 30 May 2019).

41 Gracie, C. (2019) *Equal*, London: Virago.

42 Fawcett Society (2018) 'Close the gender pay gap', *Fawcett* [Online]. Available at https://www.fawcettsociety.org.uk/close-gender-pay-gap (Accessed 23 May 2019).

43 Wisniewska, R., Ehrenberg-Shannon, B., Tilford, C. and Nevitt, C. (2019) 'Gender pay gap: women still short-changed in the UK', *Financial Times*, 23 April [Online]. Available at https://ig.ft.com/gender-pay-gap-UK-2019/ (Accessed 23 May 2019).

44 Keneally, K. (2016) 'Quotas for women: maybe the conservative side of politics is just more misogynist', *The Guardian*, 18 July [Online]. Available at https://www.theguardian.com/commentisfree/2016/jul/18/quotas-for-women-maybe-the-conservative-side-of-politics-is-just-more-misogynist (Accessed 12 September 2018).

45 Murray, R. (2014) 'Quotas for men: reframing gender quotas as a means of improving representation for all', *American Political Science Review*, 108(3): 520–32.

46 Data drawn from Table 4.1 and Jewell, H. and Bazeley, A. (2018) 'Sex and power 2018', *Fawcett Society*, 23 April [Online]. Available at https://www.fawcettsociety.org.uk/sex-power-2018 (Accessed 23 March 2019).

47 (2015) 'Why American Women Hate Board Quotas', *The Washington Post*, 9 February [Online]. Available at https://www.washingtonpost.com (Accessed 21 February 2019).

48 Osborne, J. (2018) 'How to write more inclusive job ads that will attract candidates', *Sonovate*, 17 September [Online]. Available at https://www.sonovate.com/blog/write-inclusive-job-ads/ (Accessed 10 June 2019).

49 Spender, D. (1985) *Man Made Language*. London: Pandora, p 8.

50 Murray, R. (2014) 'Quotas for men: reframing gender quotas as a means of improving representation for all', *American Political Science Review*, 108(3): 520–32.

Chapter 5

1 Croxford, R. (2019) 'UK universities face "gagging order" criticism', *BBC News*, 17 April [Online]. Available at https://www.bbc.co.uk/news/education-47936662 (Accessed 23 March 2019).

2 Mendick, R. and Rayner, G. (2018) 'Non-disclosure agreements: everything you need to know about NDAs (and their misuse)', *The Telegraph*, 25 October [Online]. Available at https://www.telegraph.co.uk/news/0/non-disclosure-agreements-everything-need-know-ndas-misuse/ (Accessed 1 January 19).

3 Kennedy, H. (2018) *Eve Was Shamed: How British Justice Is Failing Women*, London: Chatto Windus.

4   Ahmed, S. (2017) *Living a Feminist Life*, Durham: Duke University Press.

5   Ahmed, S. (2017) *Living a Feminist Life*, Durham: Duke University Press.

6   Couldry, N. (2010) *Why Voice Matters*, London: Sage.

7   Couldry, N. (2010) *Why Voice Matters*, London: Sage.

8   Couldry, N. (2010) *Why Voice Matters*, London: Sage.

9   Orwell, G. (2003) *Animal Farm* (centennial edn), London: Penguin.

10 O'Grady, S. (2010) 'A government of straight, white, privately educated men', *The Independent*, 7 August [Online]. Available at http://www.independent.co.uk/news/uk/politics/a-government-of-straight-white-privately-educated-men-2045899.html (Accessed 26 April 2019).

11 Bates, T.R. (1975) 'Gramsci and the theory of hegemony', *Journal of the History of Ideas*, 36(2): 351–66, 353.

12 Beard, M. (2017) *Women & Power: A Manifesto*, London, London review of books: Profile; Russ, J. (2018) *How to Suppress Women's Writing*, Austin: University of Texas Press.

13 For a summary, see for example Paul, A. (2018) 'Five women who missed out on the Nobel Prize', *The Observer*, 7 October [Online]. Available at https://www.theguardian.com/science/2018/oct/07/five-women-the-nobel-prize-missed (Accessed 12 May 2019).

14 A bias against recognizing the achievements of women in science. For a wonderful children's novel on this see Irving, E. (2017) *The Matilda Effect*, London: Corgi Books.

15 Epstein, C.F. (1976) 'Sex role stereotyping, occupations and social exchange', *Women's Studies*, 3(2): 185–94.

16 Russ, J. (2018) *How to Suppress Women's Writing*, Austin: University of Texas Press.

17 Savigny, H. (2017) 'Cultural sexism is ordinary: writing and re-writing women in academia', *Gender, Work & Organization*, 24(6): 643–55.

18 Lerner, G. (1986) *The Creation of Patriarchy*, Oxford: Oxford University Press; Spender, D. (1985) *Man Made Language*, London: Pandora, p 23.

19 Criado Perez, C. (2019) *Invisible Women: Data Bias in a World Designed for Men*, London: Penguin.

20 Fortin, J. and Zraick, K. (2019) 'First all-female spacewalk canceled because NASA doesn't have two suits that fit', *The New York Times*, 25 March [Online]. Available at https://www.nytimes.com/2019/03/25/science/female-spacewalk-canceled.html (Accessed 17 April 2019).

21 Criado Perez, C. (2019) *Invisible Women: Data Bias in a World Designed for Men*, London: Penguin.

22 Spender, D. (1985) *Man Made Language*, London: Pandora.

23 Spender, D. (1985) *Man Made Language*, London: Pandora.

24 Caudwell, J. (2018) 'Why this football tournament should be called the men's World Cup', *The Conversation*, 25 June [Online]. Available at http://theconversation.com/why-this-football-tournament-should-be-called-the-mens-world-cup-98348 (Accessed 31 May 2019).

25 Spender, D. (1985) *Man Made Language*, London: Pandora, p 23.

26 King, A. (2004) 'The prisoner of gender: Foucault and the disciplining of the female body', *Journal of International Women's Studies*, 5(2): 29–39.

27 Solnit, R. (2014) *Men Explain Things to Me*, Chicago: Haymarket Books.

28 King, A. (2004) 'The prisoner of gender: Foucault and the disciplining of the female body', *Journal of International Women's Studies*, 5(2): 29–39, 31.

29 Jane, E.A. (2014) '"Your a ugly, whorish, slut"', *Feminist Media Studies*, 14(4): 531–46.

[30] Citron, D. (2009) 'Law's expressive value in combating cyber gender harassment', *Michigan Law Review*, 108(3): 373–415.

[31] Mantilla, K. (2015) *Gendertrolling: How Misogyny Went Viral*, Santa Barbara: Praeger.

[32] Sest, N. and March, E. (2017) 'Constructing the cyber-troll: psychopathy, sadism, and empathy', *Personality and Individual Differences*, 119: 69–72.

[33] Reilly, C. (2016) '"Not just words": online harassment of women an "epidemic"', *CNet*, 7 March [Online]. Available at https://www.cnet.com/news/not-just-words-online-harassment-of-women-epidemic-norton-research/ (Accessed 2 May 2019).

[34] Duggan, M. (2017) 'Online harassment 2017', *Pew Research* Center, 11 July [Online]. Available at http://www.pewinternet.org/2017/07/11/online-harassment-2017/#fn-19049-2 (Accessed 2 May 2019).

[35] Adam, A. and Green, E. (2001) *Virtual Gender*, Florence: Routledge Ltd.

[36] Banet-Weiser, S. and Miltner, K.M. (2016) '#MasculinitySoFragile: culture, structure, and networked misogyny', *Feminist Media Studies*, 16(1): 171–74.

[37] Lumsden, K. and Morgan, H. (2017) 'Media framing of trolling and online abuse: silencing strategies, symbolic violence, and victim blaming', *Feminist Media Studies*, 17(6): 926–40.

[38] Add, A. (2018) 'Woman, 26, trolled online after video of her squashing spider goes viral', *The Sun*, 28 September [Online]. Available at https://www.thesun.co.uk/news/7371463/woman-trolled-spider-video-squash-county-armagh-ireland/ (Accessed 25 March 2019).

[39] Okundaye, J.O. (2017) 'The "decolonise" Cambridge row is yet another attack on students of colour', *The Guardian*, 25 October [Online]. Available at https://www.theguardian.com/commentisfree/2017/oct/25/decolonise-cambridge-university-row-attack-students-colour-lola-olufemi-curriculums (Accessed 21 March 2019).

[40] Ponsford, D. (2017) 'Telegraph corrects story saying Cambridge University would drop white authors from reading lists', *Press Gazette*, 26 October [Online]. Available at https://www.pressgazette.co.uk/telegraph-corrects-story-saying-cambridge-university-would-drop-white-authors-from-reading-lists/ (Accessed 14 April 2019).

[41] Anderson, M. (2013) 'As the Trayvon Martin case goes to trial, remembering a major media event', *Pew Research Center*, 10 June [Online]. Available at https://www.pewresearch.org/fact-tank/2013/06/10/as-the-trayvon-martin-case-goes-to-trial-remembering-a-major-media-event/ (Accessed 1 May 2019).

[42] Journalism & Media Staff and Pew Research Centre (2012) 'How blogs, Twitter and mainstream media have handled the Trayvon Martin case', *Pew Research Center*, 30 March [Online]. Available at https://www.journalism.org/2012/03/30/special-report-how-blogs-twitter-and-mainstream-media-have-handled-trayvon-m/ (Accessed 1 May 2019).

[43] Félix, D.S. (2018) 'The very American killing of Nia Wilson', *The New Yorker*, 31 July [Online]. Available at https://www.newyorker.com/culture/cultural-comment/the-very-american-killing-of-nia-wilson (Accessed 1 May 2019).

[44] Clark, M. (2016) 'Coverage of black female victims of police brutality falls short', *USA Today*, 23 April [Online]. Available at https://www.usatoday.com/story/opinion/policing/spotlight/2016/04/22/police-violence-women-media/83044372/ (Accessed 1 May 2019).

[45] AAPF, *#SayHerName* [Online]. Available at http://aapf.org/shn-campaign (Accessed 5 May 2019).

[46] Williams, S. (2015) 'Digital Defense: Black Feminists Resist Violence With Hashtag Activism', *Feminist Media Studies*, 15(2): 341–44.

47 Mendes, K., Ringrose, J. and Keller, J. (2019) *Digital Feminist Activism: Girls and Women Fight Back against Rape Culture*, Oxford and New York: Oxford University Press.

48 Mill, J.S. (1859) *On Liberty*, London: Penguin.

49 Mill, J.S. (1859) *On Liberty*, London: Penguin, p 68. Mill writes, '[t]he only purpose for which power can be rightfully exercised over any member of a civilized community, against his [sic] will, is to prevent harm to others.'

50 BBC News (2018) 'MP Jess Phillips in web plea "after 600 rape threats"', *BBC News*, 11 June [Online]. Available at https://www.bbc.co.uk/news/uk-england-birmingham-44438468 (Accessed 8 May 2019).

51 Dhrodia, A. (2018) 'Unsocial media: a toxic place for women', *IPPR Progressive Review*, 24(4): 380–7.

52 Pateman, C. (1988) *The Sexual Contract*, Stanford, Cal.: Stanford University Press, p 114.

53 Lawless, J.L., Fox, R.L. (2008) *It Takes a Candidate: Why Women Don't Run for Office*, Cambridge and New York: Cambridge University Press, p 10.

54 Spivak, G.C. (1988) *Can the Subaltern Speak?* Basingstoke: Macmillan.

55 Spivak, G.C. (1988) *Can the Subaltern Speak?* Basingstoke: Macmillan.

56 Fraser, N. (2013) *Fortunes of Feminism: From State-Managed Capitalism to Neoliberal Crisis*, Brooklyn, NY: Verso, p 21.

57 Fraser, N. (1985) 'What's critical about critical theory? The case of Habermas and gender', *New German Critique*, 35: 97–131.

58 Fraser, N. (2013) *Fortunes of Feminism: From State-Managed Capitalism to Neoliberal Crisis*, Brooklyn, NY: Verso.

59 Fraser, N. (1985) 'What's critical about critical theory? The case of Habermas and gender', *New German Critique*, 35: 97–131.

60 Gilman, C.P. (1892) *The Yellow Wall-Paper*, Boston: New England Magazine Corporation.

Chapter 6

1 *Meet the 25 White Men Who Decided to Ban Abortion in Alabama* (2019) YouTube video, added by NowThisNews [Online]. Available at https://www.youtube.com/watch?v=Wua_1AVK_RA (Accessed 1 June, 2019).

2 Firestone, S. (1970) *The Dialectic of Sex: The Case for Feminist Revolution*, London: Woman's Press; for wider discussion on this issue see for example Gerodetti, N. and Mottier, V. (2009) 'Feminism(s) and the politics of reproduction: introduction to special issue on "Feminist Politics of Reproduction"', *Feminist Theory*, 10(2): 147–52.

3 Foucault, M. (1979) *Discipline and Punish*, New York: Vintage Books.

4 Monahan, T. (ed) (2006) *Surveillance and Security: Technological Politics and Power in Everyday Life* New York and London: Routledge.

5 King, A. (2004) 'The prisoner of gender: Foucault and the disciplining of the female body', *Journal of International Women's Studies*, 5(2): 29–39, 29.

6 Manchester Metropolitan University (2014) 'MMU research reveals clothes sizing confusion', *Manchester Metropolitan University*, 6 January [Online]. Available at https://www2.mmu.ac.uk/news-and-events/news/story/?id=2256 (Accessed 3 May 2019).

7 For example, Cohen, R. and Blaszczynski, A. (2015) 'Comparative effects of Facebook and conventional media on body image dissatisfaction', *Journal of Eating Disorders*, 3(23).

8   Wolf, N. (1990) *The Beauty Myth: How Images of Beauty Are Used against Women*, London: Vintage, p 10.

9   Wolf, N. (1990) *The Beauty Myth: How Images of Beauty Are Used against Women*, London: Vintage.

10 Fardouly, J. and Vartanian, L.R. (2016) 'Social media and body image concerns: current research and future directions, current opinion in psychology, 9: 1–5.

11 Banet-Weiser, S. (2018) *Empowered: Popular Feminism and Popular Misogyny*, Durham: Duke University Press.

12 Kelly, Y., Zilanawala, A., Booker, C. and Sacker, A. (2018) 'Social media use and adolescent mental health: findings from the UK Millennium Cohort Study', *EClinicalMedicine*, 6: 59–68.

13 Banet-Weiser, S. (2018) *Empowered: Popular Feminism and Popular Misogyny*, Durham: Duke University Press.

14 Banet-Weiser, S. (2018) *Empowered: Popular Feminism and Popular Misogyny*, Durham: Duke University Press.

15 Kilbourne, J. (2013) 'The more you subtract the more you add: cutting girls down to size in advertising', in R.A. Lind (ed) *Race/Gender/Class/Media 3.0: Considering Diversity across Audiences, Content, and Producers*, Boston: Pearson, pp 179–85.

16 Tiggemann, M. and Slater, A. (2013) 'NetGirls: the Internet, Facebook, and body image concern in adolescent girls', *International Journal of Eating Disorders*, 46(6): 630–3.

17 Fardouly, J. and Vartanian, L.R. (2016) 'Social media and body image concerns: current research and future directions', *Current Opinion in Psychology*, 9: 1–5; Perloff, R.M. (2014) 'Social media effects on young women's body image concerns: theoretical perspectives and an agenda for research', *Sex Roles*, 71(11–12): 363–77; Woods, H.C. and Scott, H. (2016) '#Sleepyteens: social media use in adolescence is associated with poor sleep quality, anxiety, depression and low self-esteem', *Journal of Adolescence*, 51: 41–9.

18 Wertheim, E.H. and Paxton, S.J. (2012) 'Body image development – adolescent girls', in T. Cash (ed) *Encyclopedia of Body Image and Human Appearance*, Oxford: Academic Press, pp 187–93.

19 Hogue, J.V. and Mills, J.S. (2019) 'The effects of active social media engagement with peers on body image in young women', *Body Image*, 28: 1–5; Mills, J.S., Musto, S., Williams, L. and Tiggemann, M. (2018) '"Selfie" harm: effects on mood and body image in young women', *Body Image*, 27: 86–92.

20 Kremer, D. (2018) 'The increasing popularity of plastic surgery', *Harley St Aesthetics*, 26 January [Online]. Available at https://www.harleystreetaesthetics.com/blog/dr-kremers-blog/2018/01/26/the-increasing-popularity-of-plastic-surgery (Accessed 5 February 2019).

21 Market Research Future (2018) 'Worldwide cosmetic surgery market 2018; size, statistics, revenue and trends; forecast to 2023', *Medgadget* [Online]. Available at https://www.marketresearchfuture.com/reports/cosmetic-surgery-market-3157 (Accessed 5 April 2019).

22 Sarwer, D.B., Wadden, T.A., Pertschuk, M.J. and Whitaker, L.A. (1998) 'Body image dissatisfaction and body dysmorphic disorder in 100 cosmetic surgery patients', *Plastic and Reconstructive Surgery*, 101(6): 1644–9.

23 Marsh, S. (2018) 'Doctors warn about cosmetic surgery after woman dies in Turkey', *The Guardian*, 29 August [Online]. Available at https://www.theguardian.com/uk-news/2018/aug/29/leah-cambridge-death-turkey-clinic-cosmetic-surgery-warning (Accessed 5 April 2019).

[24] Alibhai-Brown, Y. (2010) 'Why are Asian women aspiring to Western ideals of beauty?', *The Independent*, 20 November [Online]. Available at https://www.independent.co.uk/life-style/fashion/features/why-are-asian-women-aspiring-to-western-ideals-of-beauty-2136868.html (Accessed 3 May 2019).

[25] Kaw, E. (1993) 'Medicalization of racial features: Asian American women and cosmetic surgery', *Medical Anthropology Quarterly*, 7(1): 74–89.

[26] Wolf, N. (1990) *The Beauty Myth: How Images of Beauty are Used against Women*, London: Vintage, p 18.

[27] Elgot, J. (2018) 'Boris Johnson accused of "dog-whistle" Islamophobia over burqa comments', *The Guardian*, 7 August [Online]. Available at https://www.theguardian.com/politics/2018/aug/06/boris-johnsons-burqa-remarks-fan-flames-of-islamophobia-says-mp (Accessed 2 April 2019).

[28] Baig, A. (2013) 'Malala Yousafzai and the white saviour complex', *Huffington Post*, 12 September [Online]. Available at https://www.huffingtonpost.co.uk/assed-baig/malala-yousafzai-white-saviour_b_3592165.html (Accessed 3 April 2019).

[29] Whitham, B. and Ali, N. (2018) 'The unbearable anxiety of being: ideological fantasies of British Muslims beyond the politics of security', *Security Dialogue*, 49(5): 400–17.

[30] Warsi, S. (2018) 'Why we need to change the way we talk about Muslim women', *BBC Radio 4* [Online]. Available at https://www.bbc.co.uk/programmes/articles/x7GbC3ycnSqgK3H0Bryrf7/why-we-need-to-change-the-way-we-talk-about-muslim-women (Accessed 3 May 2019).

[31] Khan, M. (2019) *It's Not about the Burqa: Muslim Women on Faith, Feminism, Sexuality and Race*, London: Pan Macmillan.

[32] BBC News (2019) 'Upskirting now a crime after campaign', *BBC News*, 12 April [Online]. Available at https://www.bbc.co.uk/news/uk-47902522 (Accessed 12 April 2019).

[33] Vera-Gray, F. (2018) *The Right Amount of Panic: How Women Trade Freedom for Safety*, Bristol: Policy Press.

[34] Bates, L. (2015) *Everyday Sexism*, London: Simon & Schuster.

[35] Vera-Gray, F. (2018) *The Right Amount of Panic: How Women Trade Freedom for Safety*, Bristol: Policy Press.

[36] Bourdieu, P. (1979) 'Symbolic power', *Critique of Anthropology*, 4(13–14): 77–85.

[37] Bourdieu, P. (2001) *Masculine Domination*, Stanford, Cal.: Stanford University Press.

[38] Millett, K. (1968) *Sexual Politics*, Boston, Mass.: New England Free Press.

[39] Bourdieu, P. and Wacquant, L.J.D. (1992) *An Invitation to Reflexive Sociology*, Polity, Cambridge Original italics, p 168.

[40] Kelly, L. (1987) 'The continuum of sexual violence', in J. Hanmer and M. Maynard (eds) *Women, Violence and Social Control*, Basingstoke: Macmillan, pp 46–60, 51.

[41] Kelly, L. (1987) 'The continuum of sexual violence', in J. Hanmer and M. Maynard (eds) *Women, Violence and Social Control*, Basingstoke: Macmillan, pp. 46–60, 48.

[42] Kelly, L. (1987) 'The continuum of sexual violence', in J. Hanmer and M. Maynard (eds) *Women, Violence and Social Control*, Basingstoke: Macmillan, pp. 46–60, 49.

[43] Smith, S., Choueiti, M. and Pieper, K. (2017) *Over Sixty, Underestimated: A Look at Aging on the "Silver" Screen in Best Picture Nominated Films*, Media, Diversity, & Social Change Initiative, February [Online]. Available at https://annenberg.usc.edu/sites/default/files/2017/05/30/MDSCI_Over%20Sixty%20Underestimated%20Report%20Final.pdf (Accessed 20 May 2019).

[44] Wilson, C. (2015) 'This chart shows Hollywood's glaring gender gap', *Time*, 6 October [Online]. Available at http://time.com/4062700/hollywood-gender-gap/ (Accessed 20 May 2019).

45 Child, B. (2015) 'Maggie Gyllenhaal: At 37 I was "too old" for role opposite 55-year-old man', *The Guardian*, 21 May [Online]. Available at https://www.theguardian.com/film/2015/may/21/maggie-gyllenhaal-too-old-hollywood (Accessed 21 May 2019).

Chapter 7

1   hooks, b. (1982) *Ain't I a Woman: Black Women and Feminism*, Boston, Mass.

2   McGuire, D.L. (2010) *At the Dark End of the Street: Black Women, Rape, and Resistance – A New History of the Civil Rights Movement from Rosa Parks to the Rise of Black Power*, New York: Knopf.

3   Barker, P. (2018) *The Silence of the Girls: A Novel*, New York: Doubleday.

4   Brownmiller, S. (1975) *Against Our Will*, New York: Simon & Schuster, p15.

5   Phillips, N.D. (2016) *Beyond Blurred Lines: Rape Culture in Popular Media*, New York: Roman & Littlefield.

6   Abdulali, S. (2018) *What We Talk about When We Talk about Rape*, New York: Myrid Editions; Gay, R. (2018) *Not That Bad: Dispatches from Rape Culture*, New York: Harper Collins.

7   Banyard, K. (2010) *The Equality Illusion: The Truth about Women and Men Today*, London: Faber and Faber.

8   United Nations (2016) 'Report: Majority of trafficking victims are women and girls', *United Nations*, 22 December [Online]. Available at https://www.un.org/sustainabledevelopment/blog/2016/12/report-majority-of-trafficking-victims-are-women-and-girls-one-third-children/ (Accessed 12 September 2017).

9   United Nations (2016) 'Report: Majority of trafficking victims are women and girls', *United Nations*, 22 December [Online]. Available at https://www.un.org/sustainabledevelopment/blog/2016/12/report-majority-of-trafficking-victims-are-women-and-girls-one-third-children/ (Accessed 12 September 2017).

10 International, A. (2018) 'Sex without consent is rape. So why do only eight European countries recognise this?' *Amnesty International*, 23 April [Online]. Available at https://www.amnesty.org/en/latest/campaigns/2018/04/eu-sex-without-consent-is-rape/ (Accessed 30 October 2018).

11 England and Wales, Scotland, Northern Ireland and the Republic of Ireland, as well as Belgium, Cyprus, Luxembourg and Germany all have consent-based definitions (Amnesty International, 2018).

12 Office for National Statistics (2018) *Sexual offences in England and Wales: year ending March 2017*, 8 February [Online]. Available at https://www.ons.gov.uk/peoplepopulationandcommunity/crimeandjustice/articles/sexualoffencesinenglandandwales/yearendingmarch2017 (Accessed 30 October 2018).

13 Topping, A. and Barr, C. (2018) 'Rape prosecutions plummet despite rise in police reports', *The Guardian*, 26 September [Online]. Available at https://www.theguardian.com/law/2018/sep/26/rape-prosecutions-plummet-crown-prosecution-service-police (Accessed 30 October 2018).

14 Crown Prosecution Service (2019) *False Allegations of Rape and/or Domestic Abuse, see: Guidance for Charging Perverting the Course of Justice and Wasting Police Time in Cases involving Allegedly False Allegations of Rape and/or Domestic Abuse*, September [Online]. Available at https://www.cps.gov.uk/legal-guidance/false-allegations-rape-andor-domestic-abuse-see-guidance-charging-perverting-course (Accessed 22 November 2019).

[15] Topping, A. and Barr, C. (2018) 'Rape conviction crisis: the systemic failures that deny justice for victims', *The Guardian*, 6 October [Online]. Available at https://www.theguardian.com/membership/2018/oct/06/conviction-crisis-rape-uk-cps (Accessed 13 March 2019).

[16] Saunders, C.L. (2012) 'The truth, the half-truth, and nothing like the truth. Reconceptualizing false allegations of rape', *The British Journal of Criminology*, 52(6): 1152–71; Lisak, D., Gardinier, L., Nicksa, S.C. and Cote, A.M. (2010) 'False allegations of sexual assault: an analysis of ten years of reported cases', *Violence Against Women*, 16(12): 1318–34.

[17] Laville, S. (2014) '109 women prosecuted for false rape claims in five years, say campaigners', *The Guardian*, 1 December [Online]. Available at https://www.theguardian.com/law/2014/dec/01/109-women-prosecuted-false-rape-allegations (Accessed 30 October 2018).

[18] Laville, S. (2014) '109 women prosecuted for false rape claims in five years, say campaigners', *The Guardian*, 1 December [Online]. Available at https://www.theguardian.com/law/2014/dec/01/109-women-prosecuted-false-rape-allegations (Accessed 14 March 2019).

[19] Levitt QC, A. and Crown Prosecution Service Equality and Diversity Unit (2013) *Charging Perverting the Course of Justice and Wasting Police Time in Cases Involving Allegedly False Rape and Domestic Violence Allegations* [Online]. Available at https://www.cps.gov.uk/sites/default/files/documents/publications/perverting_course_of_justice_march_2013.pdf (Accessed 27 October 2018) p 3.

[20] Binns, D. (2017) '10 years for woman who cried rape', *Metro*, 25 August [Online]. Available at https://www.metro.news/10-years-for-woman-who-cried-rape/721881/ (Accessed 30 October 2018).

[21] Parry, H. (2016) 'Texas state trooper is indicted for perjury in Sandra Bland case', *Daily Mail*, 6 January [Online]. Available at https://www.dailymail.co.uk/news/article-3387770/Texas-state-trooper-indicted-PERJURY-case-black-police-detainee-Sandra-Bland-died-custody.html (Accessed 3 November 2018).

[22] Carter, A.-M. (2010) 'Rape lies end in jail term', *Oxford Mail*, 11 June [Online]. Available at https://www.oxfordmail.co.uk/news/8215782.rape-lies-end-in-jail-term/ (Accessed 21 May 2019).

[23] Menon, P. (1983) 'The law of rape and criminal law administration with special reference to the commonwealth Caribbean', *The International and Comparative Law Quarterly*, 32(4): 832–70.

[24] Williams, J.E. (1984) 'Secondary victimization: confronting public attitudes about rape', *Victimology*, 9(1): 66–81, 67.

[25] Suarez, E. and Gadalla, T.M. (2010) 'Stop blaming the victim: a meta-analysis on rape myths', *J Interpers Violence*, 25(11): 2010–35.

[26] Phipps, A., Ringrose, J., Renold, E. and Jackson, C. (2018) 'Rape culture, lad culture and everyday sexism: researching, conceptualizing and politicizing new mediations of gender and sexual violence', *Journal of Gender Studies*, 27(1): 1–8.

[27] Phillips, N.D. (2016) *Beyond Blurred Lines: Rape Culture in Popular Media*, New York: Roman & Littlefield.

[28] Carter, C. (1998) 'When the extraordinary becomes ordinary: everyday news of sexual violence', in C. Carter, G. Branston and S. Allan (eds) *News, Gender and Power*, London: Routledge, pp 219–32.

[29] Soothill, K. and Walby, S. (1991) *Sex Crime in the News*, London: Routledge.

[30] Boyle, K. (2005) *Media and Violence*, London: Sage.

[31] Boyle, K. (2005) *Media and Violence*, London: Sage.

32 Moorti, S. (2002) *Color of Rape: Gender and Race in Television's Public Spheres*, Albany, NY: State University of New York Press.

33 Rao, S. (2014) 'Covering rape in shame culture: studying journalism ethics in India's new television news media', *Journal of Mass Media Ethics*, 29(3): 153–67.

34 Abdulali, S. (2018) *What We Talk about When We Talk about Rape*, New York: The New Press, p 186.

35 Domestic Violence RU (2017) *Domestic Violence RU* [Online]. Available at https://domesticviolenceru.wixsite.com/domesticviolence (Accessed 5 November 2018).

36 Nolasco, S. (2019) 'Chris Watts' horrific killings of wife, daughters still haunt investigators, new doc reveals', *Fox News*, 1 June [Online]. Available at https://www.foxnews.com/entertainment/chris-watts-murders-documentary-tell-all (Accessed 31 May 2019).

37 BBC News (2019) 'Farnham puppy farm murderer John Lowe "was father figure"', *BBC News*, 28 May [Online]. Available at https://www.bbc.co.uk/news/uk-england-surrey-48436674 (Accessed 30 May 2019).

38 Boyle, K. (2005) *Media and Violence*, London: Sage.

39 Projansky, S. (2001) *Watching Rape: Film and Television in Postfeminist Culture*, New York: New York University Press.

40 Kahlor, L. and Eastin, M.S. (2011) 'Television's role in the culture of violence toward women: a study of television viewing and the cultivation of rape myth acceptance in the United States', *Journal of Broadcasting & Electronic Media*, 55(2): 215–31.

41 Brinson, S.L. (1992) 'The use and opposition of rape myths in prime-time television dramas', *Sex Roles*, 27(7–8): 359–75; Kahlor, L. and Morrison, D. (2007) 'Television viewing and rape myth acceptance among college women', *Sex Roles*, 56(11–12): 729–39.

42 Cuklanz, L.M. (2000) *Rape on Prime Time: Television, Masculinity, and Sexual Violence*, Philadelphia: University of Pennsylvania Press.

43 Bufkin, J. and Eschholz, S. (2000) 'Images of sex and rape: a content analysis of popular film', *Violence against Women*, 6(12): 1317–44.

44 Anderson, I. and Doherty, K.H. (2008) *Accounting for Rape: Psychology, Feminism and Discourse Analysis in the Study of Sexual Violence*, London: Routledge, pp 110–14.

45 Connell, N. and Wilson, C. (1974) *Rape: The First Sourcebook for Women*, New York: New American Library; Buchwald, E., Fletcher, P.R. and Roth, M. (2005) *Transforming a Rape Culture*, Minneapolis: Milkweed Editions.

46 Buchwald, E., Fletcher, P.R. and Roth, M. (2005) *Transforming a Rape Culture*, Minneapolis: Milkweed Editions, p xi.

47 Penny, L. (2013) 'Laurie Penny on Steubenville: this is rape culture's Abu Ghraib moment', *New Statesman*, 19 March [Online]. Available at https://www.newstatesman.com/laurie-penny/2013/03/steubenville-rape-cultures-abu-ghraib-moment (Accessed 4 November 2016).

48 Levy, A. (2013) 'Trial by Twitter', *The New Yorker*, 29 July [Online]. Available at https://www.newyorker.com/magazine/2013/08/05/trial-by-twitter?subId1=xid:fr1574665188866bee (Accessed 12 April 2019).

49 Dao, J. (2009) 'Ex-soldier gets life sentence for Iraq Murders', *The New York Times*, 21 March [Online]. Available at https://www.nytimes.com/2009/05/22/us/22soldier.html (Accessed 28 April 2019).

50 CNN International.com (2006) 'Soldier: "Death walk" drives troops "nuts"', *CNN International.com*, 9 August [Online]. Available at http://edition.cnn.com/2006/WORLD/meast/08/08/iraq.mahmoudiya/index.html (Accessed 2 April 2019).

51 BBC News (2018) 'Focus on violent crime not misogyny, says police chief', *BBC News*, 1 November [Online]. Available at https://www.bbc.co.uk/news/uk-46053069 (Accessed 6 December 2018).

52 Bjornstrom, E.E.S., Kaufman, R.L., Peterson, R.D. and Slater, M.D. (2010) 'Race and ethnic representations of lawbreakers and victims in crime news: a national study of television coverage', *Social Problems*, 57(2): 269–93.

53 Powell, K.A. (2011) 'Framing Islam: an analysis of U.S. media coverage of terrorism since 9/11', *Communication Studies*, 62(1): 90–112.

54 Enloe, C. (2000) *Bananas, Beaches and Bases: Making Feminist Sense of International Politics*, Berkeley Cal., London: University of California Press.

55 Kumar, D. (2004) 'War propaganda and the (AB)uses of women', *Feminist Media Studies*, 4(3): 297–313.

56 Stabile, C.A. and Kumar, D. (2005) 'Unveiling imperialism: media, gender and the war on Afghanistan', *Media, Culture & Society*, 27(5): 765–82; Stabile, C.A. and Kumar, D. (2005) 'Unveiling imperialism: media, gender and the war on Afghanistan', *Media, Culture & Society*, 27(5): 765–82.

57 Brownmiller, S. (1975) *Against Our Will*, New York: Simon & Schuster.

58 Tanaka, Y. (2003) *Japan's Comfort Women: Sexual Slavery and Prostitution During World War II and the US Occupation*, London and New York: Routledge.

59 Blakemore, E. (2019) 'The brutal history of Japan's "comfort women"', *History*, 21 July [Online]. Available at https://www.history.com/news/comfort-women-japan-military-brothels-korea (Accessed 28 April 2019).

60 del Zotto, A.C. (2002) 'Weeping women, wringing hands: how the mainstream media stereotyped women's experiences in Kosovo', *Journal of Gender Studies*, 11(2): 141–50.

61 Nordstrom, C. (1996) 'Rape: politics and theory in war and peace', *Australian Feminist Studies*, 11(23): 147–62.

62 Sharlach, L. (2000) 'Rape as genocide: Bangladesh, the Former Yugoslavia, and Rwanda', *New Political Science*, 22(1): 89–102.

63 Power, M. (2007) 'Digitized virtuosity: video war games and post-9/11 cyber-deterrence', *Security Dialogue*, 38(2): 271–88.

64 Beck, V.S., Boys, S., Rose, C. and Beck, E. (2012) 'Violence against women in video games: a prequel or sequel to rape myth acceptance?' *J Interpers Violence*, 27(15): 3016–31.

Chapter 8

1 Wood, H. (2019) 'Fuck the patriarchy: towards an intersectional politics of irreverent rage', *Feminist Media Studies*, 19(4): 609–15.

2 Greer, G. (1971) *The Female Eunuch*, New York: McGraw-Hill, p 263.

3 Lorde, A. (1984) *Sister Outsider: Essays and Speeches*, Trumansburg, NY P151: Crossing Press.

4 Boyle, K. (2020) *#MeToo, Weinstein and Feminism*, London: Palgrave.

5 Manne, K. (2018) *Down Girl: The Logic of Misogyny*, New York: Oxford University Press.

6 Siddiqui, S. (2018) 'Kavanaugh's angry testimony raises doubts over future impartiality', *The Guardian*, 3 October [Online]. Available at https://www.theguardian.com/us-news/2018/oct/02/kavanaugh-impartial-justice-testimony (Accessed 6 June 2019).

[7]   Cooper, B. (2018) *Eloquent Rage: One Black Feminist's Refusal to Bow Down*, St Martin's Press; Chemaly, S.L. (2018) *Rage Becomes Her: The Power of Women's Anger*, New York: Atria Books.

[8]   Wood, H. (2019) 'Fuck the patriarchy: towards an intersectional politics of irreverent rage', *Feminist Media Studies*, 19(4): 609–15.

[9]   Greer, G. (1971) *The Female Eunuch*, London: MacGibbon and Kee; NHS (2017) 'Overview: female genital mutilation (FGM)', *NHS* [Online]. Available at https://www.nhs.uk/conditions/female-genital-mutilation-fgm/ (Accessed 6 June 2019).

[10] Smith-Spark, L. (2004) 'How did rape become a weapon of war?' *BBC News* [Online]. Available at http://news.bbc.co.uk/1/hi/4078677.stm (Accessed 6 June 2019).

[11] Kay, J.B. and Banet-Weiser, S. (2019) 'Feminist anger and feminist respair', *Feminist Media Studies*, 19(1): 1–7.

[12] Mullany, L. and Trickett, L. (2018) *Misogyny Hate Crime Evaluation Report,* June [Online]. Available at http://www.nottinghamwomenscentre.com/wp-content/uploads/2018/07/Misogyny-Hate-Crime-Evaluation-Report-June-2018.pdf (Accessed 6 June 2019).

[13] BBC News (2018) 'Misogyny hate crime pilot "shocking"', *BBC News*, 9 July [Online]. Available at https://www.bbc.co.uk/news/uk-england-nottinghamshire-44740362 (Accessed 6 June 2019).

[14] Morgan, R. (1970) *Sisterhood is Powerful: An Anthology of Writings from the Women's Liberation Movement*, New York: Random House.

[15] Oakley, A. (1981) 'Interviewing women: a contradiction in terms', in H. Roberts (ed) *Doing Feminist Research*, London: Routledge & Kegan Paul, pp 30–61.

[16] McIntosh, P. (1988) 'White privilege and male privilege: a personal account of coming to see correspondences through work in women's studies', in M.L. Anderson and P.H. Collins (eds) *Race, Class and Gender: An Anthology*, Belmont, CA: Wadsworth, pp 76–87.

[17] Hill Collins, P. (1990) *Black Feminist Thought Knowledge, Consciousness, and the Politics of Empowerment*, New York and London: Routledge.

[18] hooks, b. (2000) *Feminism is for Everybody: Passionate Politics*, London: Pluto Press.

[19] McGuire, D.L. (2010) *At the Dark End of the Street: Black Women, Rape, and Resistance – A New History of the Civil Rights Movement from Rosa Parks to the Rise of Black Power*, New York: Knopf.

[20] Cooper, B. (2018) *Eloquent Rage,* New York: St Martin's Press.

[21] Wood, H. (2019) 'Fuck the patriarchy: towards an intersectional politics of irreverent rage', *Feminist Media Studies*, 19(4): 609–15.

[22] Gann, R. (2021) *Critique and Utopia: Introducing Feminist Theory*, London: Palgrave Macmillan.

[23] Hemmings, C. (2011) *Why Stories Matter: The Political Grammar of Feminist Theory*, Durham and London: Duke University Press.

[24] Ahmed, S. (2017) *Living a Feminist Life*, Durham: Duke University Press.

Index